TODAY...

... an Encouraging 7/70 Journey
Hebrews 3:13
Journey 1

Sandy Picek

Denton, Texas

TODAY... an Encouraging 7/70 Journey - Life Journey Series - Journey 1

Copyright 2020 Sandy Picek

All rights reserved. No part of this publication may be reproduced, stored in a retrieval system, or transmitted in any form or by any means-electronic, mechanical, photocopy, scanning, or other – except for brief quotations in printed reviews, without the prior written permission of the publisher.

Published by Prodigal Publishing

Unless otherwise indicated, all Scripture quotations are taken from *THE MESSAGE*, copyright © 1993, 2002, 2018 by Eugene H. Peterson. Used by permission of NavPress. All rights reserved. Represented by Tyndale House Publishers, a Division of Tyndale House Ministries.

Scriptures taken from the Holy Bible, New International Version®, NIV®. Copyright © 1973, 1978, 1984, 2011 by Biblica, Inc.™ Used by permission of Zondervan. All rights reserved worldwide. www.zondervan.com The "NIV" and "New International Version" are trademarks registered in the United States Patent and Trademark Office by Biblica, Inc.™

Scripture quotations marked (NLT) are taken from the Holy Bible, New Living Translation, copyright ©1996, 2004, 2015 by Tyndale House Foundation. Used by permission of Tyndale House Publishers, a Division of Tyndale House Ministries, Carol Stream, Illinois 60188. All rights reserved.

Scripture quotations marked (TLB) are taken from The Living Bible copyright © 1971. Used by permission of Tyndale House Publishers, a Division of Tyndale House Ministries, Carol Stream, Illinois 60188. All rights reserved.

ISBN- : 978-1-7355383-1-0

Printed in the United States of America

Cover Illustration by: Sandy Picek

What you hold in your hand is what I call "an Encouraging 7/70 journey." It is a different type of journal, or journey, that you can walk through for 70 days and only 7 minutes a day.

Every Journey Date has a true life story, along with encouraging words from God.

There are 70 "journey dates" and at the end of each story, there are 3 questions to think about. You can jot down how something on a given day has touched your heart or impacted you.

We are told, "*But encourage one another daily, as long as it called Today, so that none of you may be hardened by sin's deceitfulness.*"- Hebrews 3:13. My hope is that you will be encouraged by these stories, and feel the touch of Jesus as you read them.

Blessings over you today!

Joyfully in Him,
Sandy

*For the many who inspired these stories, but especially to my husband Bill, who loves Jesus and stands by my side here on earth.
And of course Jesus, where would I be without Him!*

Journey Date 1 _____

Have you ever made a promise to someone? I imagine if you are reading this, then the answer would be yes. There are all kinds of promises. Of course the first one that I think of is my marriage vow or promise. I made a vow before God, friends, family and my husband that I would stay with him until "death do us part." I can tell you, there have been times that I thought that might not happen and then my promise would be ended. (Obviously it is not God's plan for us to be apart yet.) But, there are many other promises. What about a credit card, or a car note or a mortgage - you made a promise to that company that you would pay back the money that was borrowed. You signed your name on a dotted line and said, "Yes, I promise to pay you back what I owe you, plus interest." Or how about the many promises parents make to their children, especially when they are small. I remember my kids asking, "Mommy, can we go get ice-cream <u>later</u> if I help out around the house?"... My response... "sure honey, that's a great idea." Then <u>later</u> comes and goes and we never make it to the ice-cream store. Or the best one yet I would says to my kids, "I promise after school today we will go and _____ "(fill in the blank). And guess what, we never make it to the fill in the blank space.

As most promises are meant to be kept, and are said in good faith, sometimes they just get broken or are not kept. I imagine if you asked my children today how many promises did I make and NOT keep, they could give you a long record of them. I hate to admit that on myself, but, no point in trying to hide it - I think we have all fallen short of keeping a promise or two.

As I was thinking about this, my mind was flooded with many promises that God made to us. So many that I would be sitting here typing for probably 30 days and still not get them all listed. But there is one that has stuck out in my mind... *Isaiah 49:15 & 16 ... "Can a woman forget her child, and not have compassion on her son? Surely they may forget, Yet, I will not forget you, See, I have inscribed you on the palms of My hands..."*

Look down at your hands --- go ahead, look at them. Can you imagine if those were God's hands - YOUR NAME is indelibly carved into those hands. That is HIS promise to you. Whenever He opens up His palms He sees your name written there. I imagine it is like a scar that will never go away because He doesn't want it to. What an incredible promise - one that will never be taken back or not fulfilled. My beloved friend, let His hands reach out to you today and show you His love and your name that He has tattooed on His hands.

Today, remember as you look at your hands, that the Father sees your name inscribed in His.

****

ASK YOURSELF:

What is God revealing to me today?

_____
_____
_____
_____
_____
_____

How do I see God working in my life today?

_____
_____
_____
_____
_____

What can I do to bring a blessing to someone else?

_____
_____
_____
_____
_____

Journey Date 2 _____

On one of my trips for work, I was traveling to Wisconsin. The job started at 5:00 am, and if all went well, it would end by early afternoon. It was one of those days that I had a couple of extra daylight hours after work, so I decided to go and find a real Wisconsin Cheese Factory. With the help of the internet and my husband, we found one that was family owned for over 100 years, and it wasn't too far from where I was staying. Beechwood Cheese Factory, sounded like a winner.

I drove for approximately an hour, hoping to locate this little cheese factory, listening to the Garmin telling me where to turn. When the car finally landed to "the destination", I was parked in front of a farm house. Nope, that wasn't the cheese factory. I plugged in a different route, and off the Garmin took me, only to come upon a dead end road. It is now an hour and a half later, and still, no cheese factory. One more try in the Garmin, and while driving down the road, there is a sign that shows "9 miles to Beechwood" with an arrow pointing in the direction of the town. Confident that this is taking me to right place, there was a road block ahead that states, "road closed – turn around-no thru traffic". So another 45 minutes or so, my trusty instincts take me through the winding country roads… only to find … nothing! Dusk was about to set in, so I decided to head back to the hotel and skip the cheese factory.

Disappointment started to take over, then, just as sure as the disappointment crept in, the sun light landed on a beautiful hillside where sheep were grazing. As strange as this may sound, it was almost as if the sheep were glowing. Driving a little further was a magnificent view of an old rustic barn, with tall flowers growing all around it. I imagine the stories that could be told about this barn were amazing. Continuing the drive my eyes were filled with spectacular sights. How in the world did I miss all of this? I didn't remember any of it. My "vision" was so focused on something else that I completely drove past this beautiful country.

It is so easy to pass by God's beauty when we are in a hurry. *Psalm 143: 13 says: "Let them praise the name of the Lord for His name alone is exalted; His splendor is above the Earth and the Heavens."*

Today, take a moment and look around you, and see the spectacular things that God has placed in front of you, and breathe in His goodness.

****

ASK YOURSELF:

What is God revealing to me today?
_____
_____
_____
_____
_____
_____
_____

How do I see God working in my life today?
_____
_____
_____
_____
_____
_____
_____

What can I do to bring a blessing to someone else?
_____
_____
_____
_____
_____
_____
_____

Journey Date 3 _____

Spring is always so fun, it is a time to plant seeds, or seedlings, to watch the bushes and trees bloom and the buds open up. It is a time of anticipation. We can't wait to see the rose bush or gardenia bush produce the first bud. Then we wait for that bud to blossom and become the beautiful, fragrant flower that it was created to be. Yet before it can become that wonderful flower, that bush had to struggle through the winter and the freezing rain and cold weather. The leaves die off, there are no buds, and the branches almost appear dead. This once fragrant beauty has now suffered harsh and inclement weather. But, we believe that when springtime comes, the rains will fall and the sun will shine upon the bush and the veins of that bush will be filled with new life. Then we see it, the bud appears, and behold, a new beauty.

You and I are like this bush. Do you realize that trials entrusted to you are like a closed bud of a flower? The "inclement weather", and difficult trials, are preparing that bud to form and then to bloom where it is planted. Then when we are brought into the sunshine of His presence, the flower opens to reveal the unique design for which God created it. When we run to God in the difficult times, and stand in His Presence, He takes those trials and molds us out of them. This is what Paul meant when he said in *Romans 5:3-5,* "... *"that we rejoice in our suffering, because we know that suffering produces perseverance; perseverance produces character; and character produces hope. And hope does not disappoint us, because God has poured out His love into our hearts by the Holy Spirit whom He has given us."*

This experience of how God develops us in a particular suffering and brings us through it, richer than before, causes us to hope. The hope that God will turn suffering to blessing is never diminished.

Today, whatever "inclement weather" you have been through, or are going through now, know that God is pouring out His Presence and asking you to come stand in His sunshine, and those trials will be turned into a place of hope.

****

ASK YOURSELF:

What is God revealing to me today?

_____
_____
_____
_____
_____
_____
_____

How do I see God working in my life today?

_____
_____
_____
_____
_____
_____
_____

What can I do to bring a blessing to someone else?

_____
_____
_____
_____
_____
_____
_____

Journey Date 4 _____

Not long ago we had a power outage at our house. Of course what that means is nothing electrical is working. No lights, no fans, no heater, no telephones, no radios or televisions. Nothing, but silence. If you only have to wait a few minutes it's no big deal, but, when it's an hour, two hours, 4 hours, and through the night, the silence can be deafening. How in the world can silence be SO loud?! Even though we had our cell phones, there is still something about sitting in a still and silent home. The only noise you hear is the wind blowing, or the rain falling. Or the cats wondering around meowing. But the everyday "noise" is gone, and the silence prevails. The anticipation of "when will the silence end", grows. I've learned in the silence, that it gives my husband and myself an opportunity to just sit with each other. Sometimes we share about things, sometimes we just sit and hold each other's hand. We wait with each other, anticipating the quietness, knowing that something good is coming.

How many times have you had to wait on something? I imagine we could all make a long list of what we have waited for, or may even currently be waiting for. How many prayers have you prayed asking that question, "why Lord?" or "what now Lord?" I certainly don't have answers to those simple, but complex questions, but I can tell you that when we are waiting for an answer, HIS silence is necessary. It builds anticipation for what is about to come. In the book of Revelation, "the Lamb" comes to throne room to open the Seals. With the first 6 Seals there is noise and celebrations, but, when He opens the 7th Seal, all falls silent. *Rev. 8:1 says this – "When the Lamb opened the 7th Seal there was complete silence in Heaven for about half an hour."* Can you imagine that? Heaven will be silent! No singing, no dancing, no celebrations. That tells me that when our Lord has something so important to show us, there may be a long period of silence. He is preparing us for something great and wonderful, we just have to wait in HIS silence. Sit with Him. Hold His hand. Anticipate what HE is going to unfold, because good is coming.

Today, if you are waiting in silence for an answer, I encourage you to just wait. Tell Him, "You're all I want in Heaven, You're all I want on Earth! I want to be in the very presence of You Lord and be refreshed with Your goodness, and I will wait with You." His goodness is coming!

****

ASK YOURSELF:

What is God revealing to me today?

_____
_____
_____
_____
_____
_____
_____

How do I see God working in my life today?

_____
_____
_____
_____
_____
_____
_____
_____

What can I do to bring a blessing to someone else?

_____
_____
_____
_____
_____
_____
_____

Journey Date 5 _____

Do you know someone who speaks multiple languages? It is fascinating to me to hear people talk in a language that I don't understand. There seems to be some mysterious and intriguing wonderment about the sound of the language, and a longing to know what the person is actually saying. My previous boss spoke five different languages…German, Dutch, Flemish, Afrikaans and of course English. For grins and fun, when it was someone's birthday at work, he would sign the department birthday card, and write something in a different language. I don't know what he wrote, but I am sure that he was writing something along the lines of "happy birthday". My boss and I spoke frequently about different tasks and duties at work. If he started the conversation in Deutsch, I would probably look like one of those deer in the headlights. However, he always spoke to me in English, so that we could have a conversation together. He spoke, I listened. I spoke, he listened.

Several people have asked the question, "How do you know when God speaks? I just don't hear Him and it seems pretty foreign to me." My answer isn't very philosophical, it is simply, God speaks in a way that we hear and understand Him. He knows what ways touch our hearts and move our spirit. When we open His Word, we must simply ask Him to show us what He wants us to hear and know. Then we must be still and listen. Listen for that still small voice of the Holy Spirit. Sometimes He speaks to our heart directly from His Word, sometimes He speaks while listening to a song, or standing in a field as the wind blows. He will speak to us in different ways, but when we have ears to hear Him, and our hearts open, His voice is clear. Jesus says in *John 10:27 – "My sheep listen to My voice. I know them, and they follow Me."*

When was the last time that you felt you heard the voice of the Lord speaking to you? Do you feel that He is speaking another language and you just can't hear Him?

Today, ask Him to speak clearly to you. Open His Word and let His Spirit guide you to where He wants you be. He is waiting for the conversation… He speaks, you listen… You speak, He listens.

✳✳✳

ASK YOURSELF:

What is God revealing to me today?
_____
_____
_____
_____
_____
_____
_____
_____

How do I see God working in my life today?
_____
_____
_____
_____
_____
_____
_____
_____

What can I do to bring a blessing to someone else?
_____
_____
_____
_____
_____
_____
_____

Journey Date 6 _____

On the way in to work one morning I was suddenly stopped by screaming sirens. A fire engine and ambulance pulled out of their station and onto to the road in front of me. Someone must have called 9-1-1. I watched as they drove by and wondered where they were going. Just as quickly as I wondered, I saw the accident, just a few yards in front of me. The fire engine parked in the middle of the road to stop oncoming traffic to protect the vehicles involved - and the ambulance parked a few feet from the fire engine, closer to where the people, who were involved in the accident. I watched the firemen and emergency medical technicians go to work quickly on the scene. They went right to the problem to help and rescue the people who were in need. They stopped other vehicles from driving through the accident so no one else would be hurt.

I thought for a moment and realized that God is the same way with us. He runs to our rescue in our greatest times of need. He stops everything around us to get close to us. He waits to hear us call out to Him. He brings us His presence to give us comfort.

When you are in a time of need and you feel like you need to be rescued, remember *Psalm 61: "Hear my cry O God, attend to my prayer. From the end of the earth I will cry to You. When my heart is overwhelmed lead me to You, the Rock, that is higher than I. - Rescue me."*

Today, if you are in a time of suffering or pain, call 9-1-1 to God, Your Daddy. He listens, He comes quickly and rescues His children. He is waiting for the call.

****

ASK YOURSELF:

What is God revealing to me today?

_____
_____
_____
_____
_____
_____
_____
_____

How do I see God working in my life today?

_____
_____
_____
_____
_____
_____
_____
_____

What can I do to bring a blessing to someone else?

_____
_____
_____
_____
_____
_____
_____

Journey Date 7 _____

Our country has many enemies who assault us or at least have tried to. When the attack on 9/11 happened, I thought about the words of our President and how he talked about the enemy of our country and of this world. Then as I was reading, God placed two scriptures in front of me.

"Be self-controlled and alert. Your enemy the devil prowls around like a roaring lion looking for someone to devour." - 1 Peter 5:8 and *"The weapons we fight with are not the weapons of the world. On the contrary, they have divine power to demolish strongholds."* - 2Cor. 10:4

I started thinking about my enemy. As the word states, the devil (enemy) prowls around "like" a roaring lion. If you study the habits of lions you will find that the oldest lion is the one with the loudest roar. He will sit on one side of a clearing and the young lions will wait on the other side, waiting for the "loud roar", and then the prey will run into the very trap the old lion has set. Yes, the lion may sound and be a powerful foe, but I also think of him as old and toothless. As I pondered the idea of my enemy being "like" a lion and "not" a lion it made me realize that our enemy likes to roar loudly hoping to paralyze God's children with fear so that we might run right into the very traps we are trying to resist.

Have you ever felt like you were prey to something? Do you feel like today you are the "food" for the lion? That is where the second part comes in... "the weapons we fight with are not the weapons of the world..." You have the Lion of Judah on your side. When you are in a battle zone, or feel like "food" and are about to be devoured, remember God's word is powerful. Call out to the Lion of Judah, <u>HE</u> is able to accomplish anything on your behalf.

Today, my hope for you is that you are not in fear of an enemy who has no power, but stand in faith of the power of your Savior!

****

ASK YOURSELF:

What is God revealing to me today?

_____
_____
_____
_____
_____
_____
_____

How do I see God working in my life today?

_____
_____
_____
_____
_____
_____
_____

What can I do to bring a blessing to someone else?

_____
_____
_____
_____
_____
_____
_____

Journey Date 8 _____

Once I mailed a letter to a friend. I stuffed everything in the envelope and then as most of us do, I licked the flap and sealed the envelope. I wrote my return address on the outside of the envelope, stuck the stamp on it, was just about to take it to the mail box and remembered…. "Oh no, I forgot to put something in there!" By now the "glue" on the seal was stuck! No un-sealing it. I gently pulled on the envelope, trying not to tear it. No luck, I couldn't get the envelope opened. I wasn't at home, so I couldn't try the "steam thing" on it. So, I don't know if that really works. What was I going to do? I wanted to put something else in the envelope, but there was no way. The only thing that was a guarantee was that the letter that I sealed was going to get mailed, just like it was.

Did you know that God does the same kind of thing with us? Let me show you how I know…

Ephesians 1:13 and 14-"In Him you also trusted after you heard the word of truth, the gospel of your salvation; in whom also, having believed, you were sealed with the Holy Spirit of promise, who is the guarantee of our inheritance until the redemption of the purchased possession to the praise of HIS glory."

Isn't that something – He "seals" us with Himself, the Holy Spirit, and we are guaranteed to live in His kingdom forever. All we have to do is put our trust in Jesus, and He gives us our salvation and it is a guarantee that we are "sealed" and no one can "un-seal" us. Not even ourselves. Circumstances may seem difficult and hopeless and look like the "seal" has been broken and "other things" are trying to be "stuffed" into us… but this is God's promise… WE ARE SEALED!!!

Today, I pray that God would fill you with an abundance of His Holy Spirit, to guide you, to hold you, to give you hope but most of all to show you how much you are loved.

****

ASK YOURSELF:

What is God revealing to me today?
_____
_____
_____
_____
_____
_____
_____
_____

How do I see God working in my life today?
_____
_____
_____
_____
_____
_____
_____
_____

What can I do to bring a blessing to someone else?
_____
_____
_____
_____
_____
_____
_____
_____

Journey Date 9 _____

It was actually a Tuesday evening, which was Valentine's Day. Yep, it's that February 14th day that seems to have grown to be the most "chocolate consumption and flowers bought" day. How many of us get the chocolate on this day? My husband is so sweet, he knew that I was losing weight and didn't want to "overdo" the chocolate, but he also knows how much I LOVE chocolate, so, he gave me a small box of them. It was just enough to give me the taste of the delicious nougats, but not too much to make me over indulge. Now my daughter on the other hand told me that she felt Valentine's Day is over rated. Her exact statement to me was, "you know, I don't know why people can't just show love to each other every day instead of waiting for one day of the year." What a true statement that is. How do we show each other the love that needs to be shared every single day?

Though my husband was thoughtful and brought me the candy, the card and the candle for Valentine's Day, he goes beyond that. He will bring me flowers when I least expect it, or when I have had a tough week. He will take me out to dinner when I have had to work long hours, or just don't feel like cooking some night. He will call me up and say, "hey let's go the movies tonight and have a date night". (Yes, even after 40+ years, we still go on dates.) I am blessed to be married to a man who can think away from the dates on the calendar and thinks with his heart and soul.

That is what our God is to us. He doesn't show us His love only one day a year… He shows us His love, every day, every hour, every minute, every second. God loved us so much, that He gave us more than chocolate and flowers. He gave us the most precious gift… His Son… *"For God so loved the world that He gave His one and only Son." – John 3:16.* WOW! I just can't imagine giving up one of my children. I would rather sacrifice myself, before sacrificing one of my own. But look at those words again… don't just skim over them… HE LOVES THE WORLD! Everyone in the world! You, me, our neighbors, people we like and people we don't like. Isn't that something to think about?

Who is it today that you feel you just can't love? Let God love them today. Let God love you today. It's HIS present to you, every single day of your life.

✶✶

ASK YOURSELF:

What is God revealing to me today?
_____
_____
_____
_____
_____
_____
_____

How do I see God working in my life today?
_____
_____
_____
_____
_____
_____
_____

What can I do to bring a blessing to someone else?
_____
_____
_____
_____
_____
_____
_____

Journey Date 10 _____

It seems so hard to believe, all of my "babies" are definitely grown up. My oldest, now 22, the "middle child", now 19 and of course "the baby", almost 18 are making those "grown up decisions". Each of them looking into their future, asking that proverbial question… "now what?" Then determining what it will take to make the plans follow through and then going forward with them. But to the surmise of my young and handsome 17 year old son, standing six feet tall, with those big brown eyes, the Monday following his graduation, he went to work to find out that he was laid off. Now mind you this eager young man had already made a spreadsheet to calculate just how much it would take to buy his first car, what the insurance payments would be, how much would he need for college, how much would he need to fill the tank up with gas, what kind of stereo could he afford after he bought his car, and on and on and on. <u>He had made plans!</u> -- only for someone else to change them.

Ever have that happen to you? Who hasn't right? We have all been there. Now my son is on a job hunt, looking once again to "fit" in that right spot. I have thought about this, there is actually someone out there right now who is looking for him, because God does have the perfect job for him, one that God has made for him, (Jeremiah 29:11) but he must "go" and make the decision to look for it. He has to apply at the Human Resource offices of many places until he comes to the right one… and then … the fit is perfect!

In Matthew 28: Jesus gives us a great job opportunity. He is looking for people like William, like me, and just like you. God has the biggest HR department, with job openings every single day. You may be asking what job it is that HE wants to fill, let me write it out … *"Therefore GO and make disciples of all nations, baptizing them in the name of the Father and of the Son and of the Holy Spirit, and teaching them to obey everything I have commanded you. And surely I AM with you always, to the very end of age."* You may be thinking, yeah, this sounds good, but it doesn't pay the bills, or get us the "things" that we want or maybe even need.

I tell you the truth as one believer to another, it doesn't matter about the monetary items here on earth. They are all so temporary. But just think if you decided to take God up on this job opportunity… WOW! – can you see it? In Heaven I mean, all of the promotions, all of the "jobs" that were filled because you talked to one person about the love of Jesus Christ, and that person talked to one person, and then that person talked to two persons and more and more and more!!! The best part about this job opening, is all it takes is be alive in Christ and just talk to people. You don't have to have a degree or be uneducated, you don't have to be rich or poor, there isn't any age limit, no gender requirements, nor any racial discrimination. It's just about you and Jesus, loving each other together - to love others. You see it is the Christ within you that gives life to others. Give someone the life opportunity to know how great it is to be a disciple of Christ.

Today beloved believers, you are on God's payroll, with the greatest benefits you could ever have!

****

ASK YOURSELF:

What is God revealing to me today?

_____
_____
_____

How do I see God working in my life today?

_____
_____
_____
_____

What can I do to bring a blessing to someone else?

_____
_____
_____
_____

Journey Date 11 _____

Have you ever made a loaf of bread from scratch? The ingredients used to make bread are pretty simple… bread flour, water, milk or powdered milk, sugar, salt and yeast. When our kids were younger (before Bread Machine days) we made bread as a family. We would mix the ingredients together, then cover the dough and let it rise. After a couple of hours, we would knead the dough and then cover it again and let it rise again. Then one more time we would knead the bread and then put it in the pan and let it rise in the pan, and then put it in the oven to rise some more and cook. Now what is pretty amazing to me is that without any of these ingredients your bread won't come out like a loaf of bread, it may come out flat, or hard as rock. Of course after the Bread Machine arrived on the market, my mother-in-law gave us one for Christmas. We made Peanut Butter Bread, Dill Bread, Garlic Basil Bread, Cheese Bread, Rye Bread, all kinds of bread. BUT, a few times we left out the yeast. With a bread machine you didn't have to watch it to make sure the bread was rising, so it was easy to forget the yeast. Needless to say the bread was pretty sad. It was a big blob of hard dough. It was a three inch tall, 2 lb. Loaf of bread… yep, it was pretty bad. Isn't it funny how something so small as the amount of yeast that goes into bread can make such a big difference? A pastor said something that has stuck in my head… "a little leaven, leavens the whole loaf".

In life today we can be the "yeast" and add something special to someone's life. A smile, a kind word, a helping hand, a phone call, even possibly going out of your way to take someone out to dinner or take dinner to them. These can all be ways that you add something to someone else. You may be thinking that you have too much going on in your own life, and that you don't think you can be "the yeast" today. Then possibly you are someone who needs "the yeast" added to your life. Don't be afraid to ask, but also remember that giving can help calm the hurting places, and you can be "the yeast".

Ecclesiastes 4:9 tells us "Two are better than one, because they have a good return for their work." Who can you be the yeast to today?

Today, God has called you to be "the yeast", to be a little leaven in someone's life. If someone comes to your mind as you read this, pick up the phone and give them a call. They may just "knead" a little leavening.

****

ASK YOURSELF:

What is God revealing to me today?
_____
_____
_____
_____
_____
_____
_____

How do I see God working in my life today?
_____
_____
_____
_____
_____
_____
_____

What can I do to bring a blessing to someone else?
_____
_____
_____
_____
_____
_____
_____

Journey Date 12 _____

I was feeling a little down one day and a friend, at my office, gave me some flowers. They were beautiful, yellow daisies, purple carnations and small purple mums. Each day I came in to work and admired these lovely flowers. One week went by... the flowers were still in bloom. Two weeks went by... still they were full of color... the third week came and I noticed a couple of them beginning to fade and get a little droopy. The end of the fourth week and the flowers were still sitting on my desk, in the vase. The purple mums had all died now, and the carnations were beginning to turn a little brown. The yellow daisy's hadn't lost a petal yet, but were turning a little darker. I don't think I have ever had cut flowers last that long.

I wondered what God was trying to show me through my friend and these flowers and I thought of the word in Isaiah: *"The grass withers, the flowers fade, but the word of our God stands forever." vs. 40:8.* I know that probably by the end of the fourth week my flowers would probably be completely dead... BUT, no matter what, God stands strong forever.

In your moments of trials and wonderment, never forget that He is what helps you to stand.

Today, let Him hold you up, He is what will last forever.

****

ASK YOURSELF:

What is God revealing to me today?

_____
_____
_____
_____
_____
_____
_____

How do I see God working in my life today?

_____
_____
_____
_____
_____
_____
_____

What can I do to bring a blessing to someone else?

_____
_____
_____
_____
_____
_____
_____

Journey Date 13 _____

As we all know, the telephone is an amazing thing. You can pick it and call anyone else that has a telephone and talk to them, or listen to them. You can ask questions, you can be still and silent, you can laugh hysterically or cry with deep emotion. You can even yell if that is what you want to, and the person on the other end of the line can respond to you or with you, or they could even hang up on you. But I love what God has to say about "calling" Him.

"Call to Me and <u>I will</u> answer you with great and unsearchable things that you do not know." - Jeremiah 33:3

What a comforting verse. He doesn't say, "IF you call to Me, I MIGHT listen to you", or "When you call Me, if I don't like what you are saying, I will hang up on you." No, He makes it very clear, He wants us to call Him. He wants us to pick up the God phone line (prayer-communication), and talk to Him. To laugh, to cry, and even to yell if that is what we need to do, and He is willing to take the call. I also believe that He wants us to "listen" to Him, because He has things He wants to tell us, "great and unsearchable things". And the great thing about calling on His phone line, it doesn't cost you anything. No overseas charges, no long distance charges, no service charges. Just a listening ear and a willing heart.

Today, do you need to pick up the phone? Call Him, He is waiting for His phone to ring.

****

ASK YOURSELF:

What is God revealing to me today?
_____
_____
_____
_____
_____
_____
_____
_____

How do I see God working in my life today?
_____
_____
_____
_____
_____
_____
_____
_____
_____
_____

What can I do to bring a blessing to someone else?
_____
_____
_____
_____
_____
_____
_____
_____

Journey Date 14 _____

Newborn babies are amazing people. For nine months or so, the baby is growing, forming it's lifeline inside the mother's body. It has no worries. He or she is born and immediately becomes dependent on the mother or father. They really don't do much though. Eat, sleep and well, you know the last one. But how we adore them and want to hold them and see that they are taken care of. I almost think that babies know within themselves that don't have anything to worry about… someone will tend to their needs.

I had the privilege of holding my niece's three month old son. His eyes moved and then focused on things above him, like the ceiling fan. I wondered, "what is he thinking?", and why don't we remember what we saw or thought as babies? Did we just believe that we would be taken care of? Well, baby David got a little hungry and his mommy fed him, and he became very content… back to that place of no worries. He knew he was cared for. He knew he was safe. He knew he was loved. He had no doubts that whatever his need was, it would be taken care of.

We have a great Father who looks upon us the same way. The Psalms say it perfectly… Psalm 103:13 - *"As a father has compassion on his children, so the Lord has compassion on those who love him."* And Psalm 68:5 – *"God is the father to the fatherless, He is a defender of widows…"* . We have a great Father in Heaven who watches over us, keeps us safe, provides food and shelter for us, and wants to take our worries away. Matthew 6:25-34 is a reminder to me that we really don't need to worry, because He is taking care of us Paraphrased: *"Therefore I, Jesus, tell you, do not worry about your life, what you will eat or drink' or about your body, or what you will wear. Do not worry about tomorrow because it has enough worries of it's own. If I take care of the birds of the air and the lilies of the field, and I love you much more than these, then I will take care of you. Do not worry, but follow Me, and seek Me, I will take care of you."*

Today my beloved, are you worried? Be like baby David, and trust in the greatest parent of all… God our Father.

****

ASK YOURSELF:

What is God revealing to me today?

_____
_____
_____
_____
_____
_____
_____
_____

How do I see God working in my life today?

_____
_____
_____
_____
_____
_____
_____
_____

What can I do to bring a blessing to someone else?

_____
_____
_____
_____
_____
_____
_____
_____

Journey Date 15 _____

Years ago my son joined the Army National Guard when he was 20. While he was in Basic Training we were surprised one Sunday evening with a 20 minute phone call. As we were talking, he was coughing, and breathing hard, and it sounded like there was a lot of wind in the background. Well, sure enough he was outside in the cold 10 degrees with the wind blowing behind him, but he was making the call. He said he didn't care how cold it was, he was going to take advantage of his "free time" that he "earned".

So we talked or should I say, he talked, non-stop about the happenings of boot camp and the incredible discipline that was required of the new recruits. My son was sharing about one of his "DS" (I have learned that stands for Drill Sargent) and how the DS would continually tell them "they were the worst platoon he has ever had". Of course, then the DS would share stories of war and the discipline it took to be able to be in combat and fight the enemy. The DS described discipline as knowledge. How interesting I thought.

Then there it was, plain on paper, or should I say plain as a "Proverb" right out of the New International Bible... *Proverbs 12:1 "Whoever loves discipline loves knowledge, but he who hates correction is stupid!"*

I love how the NIV Bible puts it... *he who hates correction is stupid...*ouch! I am not sure about you, but that was a stinger. My son was standing in a place of total discipline and taking on as much knowledge as he could, and yet I sat in my comfy home, drinking hot tea, snuggled under the blanket and complaining that I have to be disciplined. Let's face it, as human beings we don't like to be corrected. Yet God tells us that correction is good for us and brings us knowledge.

Today ask God to bring knowledge by your side, even if it's through discipline.

****

ASK YOURSELF:

What is God revealing to me today?

_____
_____
_____
_____
_____
_____
_____
_____

How do I see God working in my life today?

_____
_____
_____
_____
_____
_____
_____
_____

What can I do to bring a blessing to someone else?

_____
_____
_____
_____
_____
_____
_____

Journey Date 16 _____

Over the past week, I noticed that my husband and I frequently stopped to get something to drink while driving on the road. Bill loves Starbucks (like I am sure many of you do). He usually gets a "grande' mocha latte'" which I think is another name for large cup of hot coffee with whole milk that comes out foamy. Obviously you can probably tell that I don't drink coffee. My Starbucks cup is usually filled with good ole' hot chocolate with lots of whip cream on top. My daughter likes to have her Starbucks cup filled with "decaf caramel macchiato" (not sure if I even spelled that right). Now if we aren't taking a Starbucks stop, we may take a Sonic stop or Wendy's stop or "fill-up" our thirsts with something from the local gas station after we have filled up the car. It could be an ice cold root-beer, or a bottle of apple juice, or even just a plain bottle of water. We usually get something that we think will satisfy that thirst in us.

But, I love what Jesus has to tell us about being thirsty…. *"If anyone is thirsty, let him come to Me and drink. Whoever believes in Me, as the Scripture has said, streams of living water will flow from within him." – John 7:37-38*

Read it again… that is such a wonderful gift to offer us. A never ending drink. A drink that goes beyond any thirst we could ever have. HE alone will fill us with the "living water" that is unstoppable. Oh what a gracious Savior we have. How much He loves us to offer us the best thirst quenching drink we would want. Is your cup being filled with things that are not satisfying? Are you wondering where or how will your next cup be filled? Let our Jesus come and pour His living water into you.

Today take a leap of faith and let Jesus fill your cup with His living water.

****

ASK YOURSELF:

What is God revealing to me today?
_____
_____
_____
_____
_____
_____
_____
_____

How do I see God working in my life today?
_____
_____
_____
_____
_____
_____
_____
_____

What can I do to bring a blessing to someone else?
_____
_____
_____
_____
_____
_____
_____

Journey Date 17 _____

I was remembering a time when my son was little and he wanted a peanut butter and jelly sandwich. And of course a good mom wouldn't deprive her children of such a want, so I made it for him. We did have a rule in the house that you could only eat at the table. No carrying food around the house. You can imagine, a four year old carrying a PBJ sandwich around the house, right?! Then a few days later, I was laying down in my bed, with my son to get him to take his nap, then a waft of the peanut butter aroma crossed my nostrils. I thought for a moment... I knew I didn't give him peanut butter that day, where could the peanut butter smell be coming from? The headboard on my bed had "secret hiding places". There were sliding doors with little cubby holes to put nick knacks and books in. I kept mine empty, or at least I thought they were. That delightful smell of the peanut butter was really beginning to intrigue me... I had to find out where it was coming from. Yep, you guessed it, hidden in the "secret place". As I slid the door open on the headboard, there was the PBJ from days ago. My son was nice enough to leave it on the plate, but it had become hard and crusty and the bread was shriveling up to uncover the peanut butter and jelly.

I am not sure why I didn't get a whiff of the peanut butter smell before then, but God reminded me that un-forgiveness is kind of like this sandwich. You see, if you hurt someone or someone hurts you, and forgiveness is not sought as soon as possible, then you can become hard and crusty, and begin to shrivel up on the inside and the outside. I know that there are some places in our lives that are difficult to ask for forgiveness and possibly harder places in our lives that we need to forgive... but I urge you today, to seek God and let Him show you if there are any "secret places" that need to be forgiven. When we don't forgive others or forgive ourselves it will hinder our relationship with God.

Jesus said, *"For if you forgive men when they sin against you your Heavenly Father will also forgive you. But if you do not forgive men their sins, your Father will not forgive your sins." - Matthew 6: 9-14*

Today, don't let the peanut butter and jelly in your life stay hidden and bring an un-wanting aroma.

****

ASK YOURSELF:

What is God revealing to me today?
_____
_____
_____
_____
_____
_____
_____
_____

How do I see God working in my life today?
_____
_____
_____
_____
_____
_____
_____
_____

What can I do to bring a blessing to someone else?
_____
_____
_____
_____
_____
_____

Journey Date 18 _____

Have you ever been up early in the morning to see the beautiful sunrise? As I was driving in to work one day, I looked up and saw a picture of how I would describe awesome beauty! The clouds filled the sky, with a gray matter, billowing everywhere, and the sun was rising behind them, peeking through ever so slightly. As I continued to drive, the sun rose a little more, piercing through the dense, billowing clouds. The rays from the sun began bursting through the clouds. I kept driving. The sun kept rising. The sun and the rays became the focus and the clouds began to disappear. As I reached my final destination, I turned and looked one more time at the sky. The sun was almost to its brightest moment in the morning. The golden rays were breaking through the entire sky, as if they were never ending. The sun became the complete focus. It was shedding amazing light throughout the clouds and the darkness.

As I remained looking at this incredible sight, I imagined this was exactly who Christ is in our lives. He is the awesome Son rising in the midst of the darkness, breaking through the clouds of our lives, bursting into an awesome ray of joy. Psalm 16 says it like this – *"Therefore my heart is glad and my tongue rejoices; my body also will rest secure, because You, Oh God will not abandon me to the grave, nor will You let Your Holy One see decay. You have made known to me the path of life; You will fill me with Your joy in Your presence, with eternal pleasures at Your right hand."*

Today I hope that you feel His ray of presence near you and bring you the peace and joy He longs to give.

****

ASK YOURSELF:

What is God revealing to me today?
_____
_____
_____
_____
_____
_____
_____
_____
_____

How do I see God working in my life today?
_____
_____
_____
_____
_____
_____
_____
_____
_____

What can I do to bring a blessing to someone else?
_____
_____
_____
_____
_____
_____
_____

Journey Date 19 _____

I love to start projects. Any kind of project. An example of this is we were building an office space in a warehouse we are renting. We designed the space on paper, drew up the plans, determined how much supplies would be needed, approximately how long it would take for the office space to be completed and what the cost would be to finish it. We had to tear down the existing room because we were expanding. Then we purchased the materials and went to work. It was a long process in getting the office spaces finished. While building the room, we would come up with other ideas that weren't on the plan, so we changed them in mid-stream. Or we would run out of funds temporarily. Then we would hire people to help, and the work wasn't exactly like we wanted it, so we would have to tear it down and re-do it. But, we still had the vision of what the finished product will look like. One day we knew we would see it at its completion, and it will be great!

We are the same way with our God. He started you as HIS vision and project. He planned you and created you and has plans for you along the way. Sometimes we follow His plans and go on the road that He chooses for us. Sometimes we take a detour and hang out with "other people" to help us in life and the help isn't so great, so He has to re-do our path for us.

His word tells us "*being confident of this that HE who began a good work in you, will carry it to completion until the day of Christ Jesus.*" - Philippians 1:6. Do not doubt today that HE, our Lord has a perfect plan for you and that HE will bring it to completion. You are His vision and each day He is working in your life.

Today, trust Him to work on His most precious and beautiful project -- YOU!

****

ASK YOURSELF:

What is God revealing to me today?

_____
_____
_____
_____
_____
_____
_____
_____

How do I see God working in my life today?

_____
_____
_____
_____
_____
_____
_____
_____
_____

What can I do to bring a blessing to someone else?

_____
_____
_____
_____
_____
_____
_____
_____

Journey Date 20 _____

One morning it was really cold. Probably around the 32 degree mark. As I was driving to work at my usual 6:45 am, I noticed it was difficult to see through the front window. It had that dirty film on it from the pollen blowing. Not thinking much about it, I hit the window washer fluid to clean off the dirt film, and did I get a BIG shock. The fluid froze on the window. The wipers kept going, but I couldn't see a thing. Since the sun was not up yet, the frozen window washer fluid was completely impossible to see through. The truck wasn't warm enough yet to thaw out the frozen window, so all I could think to do was get off of the road as quickly as possible. It was only a short distance to get to a safe place off of the beaten path, but the road had only two curvy lanes. My heart raced for a few moments as I searched for the first turn off. Finally, I reached the safe place where I could sit and wait for the defroster to heat up, and melt the frozen liquid off of the window. After a couple of minutes, the window was clear, and the road was easy to see. So the journey to work continued safely.

How quickly it was that I could not see out the front window of the truck. It was really scary. But life is that way also. We can be traveling down a road of life, not really thinking about where we are going, or how we are getting there, and all of a sudden we are in a place that we wonder - "how in the world did we get here?" Why couldn't I see what God was trying to show me? How could I let myself get to a place that completely covered up the truth. The "dirt film" was now thick, and the "cleaning fluid" of me, taking matters into my own hands, just made it worse. Jesus always gives us options to follow Him and to let Him clean the dirt film using His precious blood. He died to cleanse us - but He rose from the grave to love and forgive us.

Matthew 26: 26-28 speaks clearly - "And as they were eating, Jesus took bread, blessed and broke it, and gave it to the disciples and said, "Take eat; this is My body." Then He took the cup, and gave thanks, and gave it to them, saying, "Drink from it, all of you. For this is My blood of the new covenant which is shed for many for the remission of sins." Jesus is the defroster. He is waiting for you to pull over and let Him breathe His warm breath of life and clear off the cloudy, frozen window.

Today is the time for celebrating the resurrection of our Savior. What is it that you want to hand to Him? He is waiting for you to pull over and lay the covered window of life in His hands.

****

ASK YOURSELF:

What is God revealing to me today?

_____
_____
_____
_____
_____
_____

How do I see God working in my life today?

_____
_____
_____
_____
_____
_____
_____

What can I do to bring a blessing to someone else?

_____
_____
_____
_____
_____
_____
_____

Journey Date 21 _____

A dear friend came back into my life after several years. Before I met up with my friend, I had great anticipation of excitement, wondering how much each of us had changed, and then I realized how much I missed talking with him. I remembered how he searched for truth, and hungered for wisdom. I forgot how much our conversations brought deeper insight to who we were on the inside. But most of all I forgot that he really had a great listening ear, and a voice to share encouragement. Then I realized as my husband and I were getting in our cars, and my friend was leaving, that I had missed out on a whole lot of sharing and caring over the past three years. Why did I wait three years to see my friend? Why did I let time steal away such a precious commodity of caring?

Then I understood, it isn't that I didn't want to visit with my friend, I just didn't do it. I made excuses. "Life" got too busy --- and there it was --- I do the very same thing with God and Jesus. So many things that I let get in the way with my "time" with "my friend". The closest friend I could ever have, Jesus! Yet, I let time just pass me by and ask those questions, like "Lord, what ARE you doing in my life?" and there He is ready to answer me, I just have to ask and then listen. Jesus is always ready to show up at the next meeting, whenever that meeting is. Three years, three months, three weeks, three days, three hours, three minutes.... It really doesn't matter to Him, He always shows up with the answer. Just pray!

Luke 3:21 & 22 "When all of the people were baptized, Jesus was baptized too. And as He was praying, Heaven was opened and the Holy Spirit descended on Him in bodily form like a dove. And a voice came from Heaven: "You are My Son, whom I love; with You I am well pleased.""

Isn't that awesome! All Jesus did was pray and Heaven was opened! All we have to do is pray and Heaven will open! Thank You Lord that the Heavens will open when we call on Your name.

Today, may you call out to Him, and the Heavens open up before you.

****

ASK YOURSELF:

What is God revealing to me today?
_____
_____
_____
_____
_____
_____
_____
_____

How do I see God working in my life today?
_____
_____
_____
_____
_____
_____
_____
_____
_____
_____

What can I do to bring a blessing to someone else?
_____
_____
_____
_____
_____
_____
_____

Journey Date 22 _____

Lately as I look in the mirror I am noticing a few more wrinkles, a few more gray hairs, but nothing that a little make-up or "tender loving care" can't take care of. The one thing though that I cannot just over look is my vision.

A few months ago we had gone out to eat and I realized that my arms were just not long enough anymore and I had to have one of my children hold the menu for me (on their side of the table) or have someone read to me off of the menu what I wanted. So, I broke down and bought me some of those "reading" glasses. You know - the 1.00+ glasses. That worked, I could read again, but I kept forgetting to bring my glasses with me when we would go out to eat, so I still had to have help, to see. Then a little more time went by and I had to graduate to the 1.25+ glasses. I thought these will last longer than the 1.00+ glasses did. So I bought myself three pairs of glasses, one for my purse, one for work and one for reading by the couch. Early one morning I was up reading and the words just didn't seem clear again. I thought well, it must be that the light is bad, since it was still dark outside. I turned up the light to help me see better – nope – I realized I was now graduating to a 1.50+ reading glasses. Surely I will stay at this level of reading glasses for quite some time, and Target had reading glasses for $1.00. What did I do, I bought 10 pair of glasses. They are sitting all over my house, in my purse, at work, you name it, there is probably a pair of reading glasses nearby. By now you can probably imagine where I am about to go with this story…. These ten pair of glasses, yeah well, let's just say that I am probably going to just skip the 1.75+ and go straight for the 2.00+'s. When I think my vision is clear, it just becomes cloudy and fuzzy again.

That is how it is with my relationship with Jesus. I go along okay, and I think yep I can see everything clearly that He wants me to see, and behold, things become cloudy and fuzzy and I have to go back and seek forgiveness, seek humility, seek "help" and look for the clarity with my relationship with Christ, and He gives me clear vision once again. There is a familiar scripture that Amy Grant put into a song … *"Thy word is a lamp unto my feet and a light unto my path."*… See it doesn't say "my word" it says *"THY WORD"* –

"God's word" is a lamp, a light a clear way to see the path that He wants me to take. When my vision gets cloudy, He makes it clear.

Today, I hope that if you have "cloudy vision" that you will seek Him and His word for the clearness that He has for you.

****

ASK YOURSELF:

What is God revealing to me today?
_____
_____
_____
_____
_____

How do I see God working in my life today?
_____
_____
_____
_____
_____
_____

What can I do to bring a blessing to someone else?
_____
_____
_____
_____
_____
_____

Journey Date 23 _____

I truly enjoy meeting someone for the first time. As you introduce yourself or someone else introduces you, there seems to be an automatic reflex to hold out your right hand and shake the other persons' hand. As you shake hands you can get a "feel" for that person. The handshake could be strong and firm, almost like a vice grip, or maybe it is soft and mushy, like a limp noodle. Or maybe it is a handshake that is warm and gentle with confidence and surety. Then there is the person whom you haven't seen in a long time. They don't just get a handshake, they get a "HANDSHAKE" with the right hand and then you throw your left arm around them and give them a big HUG! One of those hugs that says, "Man I have missed you, I am so glad to see you again!"

When God meets us for the first time I believe He gives us a handshake. One that says "I know you already and have waited for our first handshake". Then as time goes by we forget that first meeting with Him. We forget that His handshake is strong, firm, soft, warm and gentle. Then when we come back to meet Him again it is clear that He lets us know that He has missed us and throws His left arm around us and holds us tight. He does this same thing in the midst of our hurt and pain. He does this in times of joy and gladness. He just wants to share His time with you. Isaiah shows God's action so true: *"So do not fear, for I am with you; do not be dismayed, for I am your God. I will strengthen you and help you; I will uphold you with my righteous right hand. For I am the Lord, your God, who takes hold of your right hand and says to you, Do not fear; I will help you."* - Isaiah 41:10 & 13

I can imagine God grabbing your right hand to give you a great handshake and pulling you toward Him, but then I can see Him throwing His left arm around you and telling you how much He cares for you and wants you close to Him.

Today find someone you can shake hands with and let your left arm embrace them, and remember that is what God wants to do with you.

****

ASK YOURSELF:

What is God revealing to me today?

_____
_____
_____
_____
_____
_____
_____
_____

How do I see God working in my life today?

_____
_____
_____
_____
_____
_____
_____
_____

What can I do to bring a blessing to someone else?

_____
_____
_____
_____
_____
_____
_____

Journey Date 24 _____

Sometime ago a man was in a speed boat race and his boat crashed. I found out through a friend, that the "cockpit" is actually a capsule that breaks away and keeps the pilot safe. It drops to the bottom of the lake, then a "pinging" sound is sent out so that a rescue team can find the capsule. As we all know, a lake is very muddy, murky, miry and dark. Imagine after a crash how the mud gets stirred up and the lake becomes more dense.

Apparently the pilot only has a few minutes of oxygen until the water starts to seep into the capsule, so the rescue team needs to find him quickly. However, this particular pilot was under water for 15 minutes. Can you imagine what must have been going through his mind? The only thing that he saw was thick, miry, dense darkness. If there were fish in the lake, the pilot probably couldn't have even seen them. What must he have been feeling? Fear of dying in a capsule, laying on the bottom of a lake, and not have anyone around to save him? The rescue team did find him after the 15 minutes and brought him to the top of the lake. As he was being removed from the capsule, the rescue team realized that he was alive. They found the only reason he did not die was due to the helmet he had on. It was "sealed" tight around his neck, which kept the water out. He had a hope in the middle of the darkness, that his life would be saved.

We can be much like this pilot. We go full speed ahead, pouring ourselves into the world and the worldly things, and we can become captive of those things. They may take us into the dark places where we feel there is no escape, and no hope... but we do have hope... our hope, our escape is Jesus. He has the seal around our hearts. 2 *Corinthians 1:21 - 22 states it this way... "Now it is God who makes both us and you stand firm in Christ. HE anointed us, set HIS seal of ownership on us, and put His Spirit in our hearts as a deposit, guaranteeing what is to come."* Isn't that wonderful?!! God, Jesus, loves us so much that HE has already saved us from the darkest places that we may walk in. We are "sealed" in Him. In Him there is no darkness.

Today, I pray that you know, even standing in the dark places, that God is standing right next to you. Whether you are confused, frustrated, sad, lonely, whatever the place may be, He has you sealed in His love.

****

ASK YOURSELF:

What is God revealing to me today?
_____
_____
_____
_____
_____
_____

How do I see God working in my life today?
_____
_____
_____
_____
_____
_____

What can I do to bring a blessing to someone else?
_____
_____
_____
_____
_____
_____

Journey Date 25 _____

Some time ago I did something that I have never done in my 50 years of living. I dug a grave in a cemetery. I spent the day with my lifelong friend, Constance. It was a day that I believe neither of us will ever forget. We drove to East Texas and buried her mother's ashes next to her father's graveside. It was a beautiful day for us to open up the ground and place the keepsake box deep inside the hole, and then cover it with the brown earth and grass. It was so eye opening to me. The dead is physically dead, but we must remember that the spirit and soul moves on to live for eternity. Digging this grave, and then covering it up with dirt was such a symbol of burying our past, our hurts, our sins, our pains, our strongholds and our life as we breathe.

But we are still living here, today and God gives us the chance to be new every morning. We are no longer bound by the things of the earth. We can step into the joy and the freedom when we step into the presence of our Lord. Lamentations 3: 22-24 says it wonderfully ... *"The Lord's mercies and HIS compassions fail not. They are new every morning; Great is God's faithfulness. The Lord is my portion, says my soul. Therefore I hope in Him.!"*

Isn't that so wonderful...God gives us His mercies and compassions every single morning. When our soul hurts, His compassion covers us. When our body is in pain, His mercy is unending. A day will come when we will be the one with the dirt being thrown over our bodies, but until then we are given a new day, every day. My friend's mother put her hope and trust in the Lord, and she now dances in the streets of Heaven with the many who have gone before her. Do you know Him today? If someone asked you... do you know what will happen to your soul when you die, is it clear that you will be in the Heavens with our great and mighty King?

Today, my hope is that all those who can read these words, will know the new mercies and compassion of our Lord, Jesus Christ every morning.

****

ASK YOURSELF:

What is God revealing to me today?

_____
_____
_____
_____
_____
_____
_____
_____

How do I see God working in my life today?

_____
_____
_____
_____
_____
_____
_____
_____
_____
_____

What can I do to bring a blessing to someone else?

_____
_____
_____
_____
_____
_____
_____

Journey Date 26 _____

We have an overstuffed chair in our house that has a blanket draped on it. The humorous thing about this blanket is that our young kitty, Shadrach, likes to climb up under it. He gets his body about half way under it, and then stops. He freezes in that position. It is really funny to watch him do this. It is as if he is on a mission to hide himself from Samson, the big kitty. If I could get into his little cat brain, I think he would be thinking something like this: "Okay, I've hidden myself from that other Big guy (Samson) and he can't see me. As long as I stay still and don't make any noises, he will pass right by me. Then when he passes by me I can be free to go about roaming the house again." Little does our Shadrach know, that Samson is older and smarter, and Samson heads right for him. When Samson discovers that Shadrach is under the blanket, of course he has to bite on Shadrach's tail, or swat at it. The look on Shadrach's face is one of pure shock and the thought of, "you aren't supposed to see me doing this, how did you find me?"

I can tell you that I personally have done that very thing with my relationship with God. Many times I have done things that I didn't think that God could really see what I was doing. My thought process was, if I just don't tell anyone, then He won't know about it, and it really won't hurt me. I will just be quiet about it and HE won't find me. Just like Samson though, God has been around a whole lot longer than me, and He is definitely much wiser than me. Why would I think that I could hide, whatever thing it was that I was trying to hide, from God? When God saw those "things", He was kind enough not to "bite my tail", or "swat" at me. But, He would show me how I was hurting myself and my relationship with Him by hiding those "things". Many times He would speak clearly through a friend or family member. Sometimes it would be a gentle nudge through a sermon, that, "He found me". Other times He would confront me in a manner that would be pretty shocking, kind of like Samson biting Shadrach's tail. But each time I knew that God was looking out for me. He was trying to protect me.

I use to think that God really doesn't know everything about me. In *Luke 12:7 & Matthew 10: 30 &31 Jesus says, "Indeed, the very hairs on your head are all numbered. Don't be afraid; you are worth much more than many sparrows."* This little verse tells me that if God knows every hair on my head, and which number is falling out on what day, then who am I to think that I can hide anything from Him? He loves us that much. To know us so intimately that our hairs are numbered! What a thought to me!

Today if there is a place that you feel like you are hiding from God, that He will nudge you, and you will trust Him for His grace and mercy and forgiveness. Nothing is too great for our God and Savior. Trust Him with everything, since He already knows everything.

****

ASK YOURSELF:

What is God revealing to me today?
_____
_____
_____
_____
_____

How do I see God working in my life today?
_____
_____
_____
_____
_____

What can I do to bring a blessing to someone else?
_____
_____
_____
_____
_____

Journey Date 27 _____

Have you ever bought a present early for someone and had to hide it? You know, saw the perfect gift for that someone special, but it was too early to give it to them, so you put in the closet or stuck in one of your drawers, or maybe even asked a friend to hold on to it so that your "hidden" present wouldn't be found. Then the day comes when you get to give the gift to the special someone. You have anticipated this day. You just can't wait to see the look on their face. And maybe, it has been a while since even you have seen the gift, because you wrapped it up so neatly and beautifully, and you yourself are trying to remember just exactly how the gift looked. Then, when the hidden gift is opened you see the look on the special someone's face and you are reminded how much they mean to you. You are reminded that you knew exactly what to get and it brings joy to you, to see the joy that it brought to them.

Psalm 119:11 says, "I have hidden Your word in my heart, oh God, so that I may not sin against You."

I thought about this verse this morning, as I was rushing to get ready for work. Thinking, I don't have time to stop and read and pray and spend my "usual" time with the Lord. Then He reminded me of this awesome verse. He is with me always, hidden in my heart. Even if I don't stop for Him, He always stops for us and has a present ready for us to open. He is always ready to reveal the "hidden" gift of His word to us. You probably have several "hidden words gifts)" that you can recall.

Today, when you think that your walk is not close with God or you have not given Him the time that you think He wants, just look in your heart, HE has a special gift that has been hidden and when you open it, what joy it will bring you and Him.

****

ASK YOURSELF:

What is God revealing to me today?

_____
_____
_____
_____
_____
_____
_____
_____

How do I see God working in my life today?

_____
_____
_____
_____
_____
_____
_____
_____

What can I do to bring a blessing to someone else?

_____
_____
_____
_____
_____
_____
_____

Journey Date 28 _____

Lighthouses are magnificent structures. I remember traveling to Galveston Island and taking the Ferry Boat to the other side of the bay. At the shoreline was an old lighthouse. It looked pretty worn and beat up with paint chipping and peeling and rust marks all over it. During the day, Seagulls would land on the outer walkway of the lighthouse, as if they knew it was a safe place for them. The height of the lighthouse seemed to reach high above the shoreline, almost into the clouds. I wondered, did this old, worn, weather beaten lighthouse really work. How could a place that was used and deteriorated help anyone? Then the evening came and we saw the beacon of light. In the midst of the dark night, the light became stronger and stronger. All that you could see was the light and not the old, worn building.

You and I are the same way. You may feel like you are the old, worn, beat up building and there is nothing that you can offer. Christ reminds us in Matthew; *"You ARE the light of the world, a city on a hill cannot be hidden... so let your light shine." - 5; 15-16.*

Today, you are a bright and shining light to someone. Don't ever doubt that you have a reason and a purpose here. Even through your troubles and your heartaches your light is valuable. Remember, a light isn't valuable unless it is visible. So let your light shine today.

****

ASK YOURSELF:

What is God revealing to me today?

_____
_____
_____
_____
_____
_____
_____
_____

How do I see God working in my life today?

_____
_____
_____
_____
_____
_____
_____
_____

What can I do to bring a blessing to someone else?

_____
_____
_____
_____
_____
_____
_____
_____

Journey Date 29_____

So how many sports fans are out there? Football, baseball, basketball, soccer, hockey, what is your favorite sport? I must confess, I'm not a big sports fan, except when they get to the end of the game to see who wins. But, every sport out there has one thing in common…and that is to finish the game as the winning team. But in order to be the winning team, or reach the goal, sports teams have coaches and plans to make the perfect play. Sometimes those plays happen just as they were planned out. Then, there are the times that the opposing team interrupts the plan. But, the players never lose their sight of the game. They stay focused on what the goal of the game is, and that is to get to the finish line and win!

Our lives are much like the games. We make plans. We have goals. We decide when and where things should happen… but… interruptions happen. The doctor calls and says it's not good news. Your spouse comes home to tell you the company they work for is relocating. Your boss calls you into the office and starts out with, "I hate to tell you this, but we are cutting back"… and, the list could go on and on. Our plans have just been turned upside down. Life as we know it, is going in a completely different direction. But we forget what the goal is. We forget what the final prize is.

Like the team players, we must stay focused on the "goal". We must remember to trust our Lord with our "interruptions". Plans may be in place, but detours do come along. Our eyes should stay on the goal. What is that goal you may be asking… 2 Timothy 4:7-8 says it like this: *"I have fought the good fight, I have finished the race, I have kept the faith. Now there is in store for me the crown of righteousness, which the Lord, the righteous Judge, will award to me on that day, and not only to me, but also to all who have longed for His appearing"*.

Today, the plans you have made may be changed. Remember though, when you keep your eyes focused on Him, the finished goal will be the best reward you could ever ask for.

****

ASK YOURSELF:

What is God revealing to me today?
_____
_____
_____
_____
_____
_____
_____
_____

How do I see God working in my life today?
_____
_____
_____
_____
_____
_____
_____
_____

What can I do to bring a blessing to someone else?
_____
_____
_____
_____
_____
_____
_____

Journey Date 30_____

My daughters and I would watch a show called "The Wedding Dress". I know it's a girly show, but it's interesting to see what kind of wedding dress a bride to be will pick out. The one thing that I noticed is that brides no longer wear veils that cover their faces. When I got married 40 years ago, the veil was one of the most important items to wear. It had to be a veil that covered the brides face, so as she walked down the aisle, her groom was standing, waiting to see her beauty, for him alone. When the vows were finished, and the preacher says, "you may now kiss your bride", the new husband lifts her veil and sees her face for the first time as his wife. She is radiant and glowing, and as she looks at him, her radiance reflects upon him and he too has a radiance that only he can have at that moment in time. Now the veil is lifted, the couple kisses, and they are united as one. The minister has them turn around and announces to the crowd, "Introducing Mr. & Mrs. ..." As they face the crowd, their radiance is almost contagious. The glow on their faces is overflowing.

The words in 2 Corinthians 3:12-18 are similar to that of a bride and groom. Let me write it out... *"With knowing Christ we do not need to cover our faces, or have veils to cover our faces, with Christ the veil is removed and when the veil is removed we have freedom, and we with unveiled faces reflect the Lords glory, and are being transformed into His likeness with ever increasing glory, which comes from the Lord who is the Spirit."* Our God is so good to us. Like the bride, we walk daily hidden behind a veil, in our secrets, trials, troubles and tribulations. We try to cover up what we don't want others to see. We are hiding the truth, which may be painful. The great thing is that we do not have to wear a veil to cover up the problems, or let the problems take control of us. God has lifted the veil from our faces and has given us the freedom to stand in His presence and trust Him to take care of us. As we trust Him, the radiance in our faces becomes clearer. This doesn't mean the problems will go away. It just means that we can stand, reflecting God's glory, and have a contagious Spirit about us.

Let the Lord lift the veil from your face today. Look upon Him with splendor, as the groom looked upon the bride, and let His glory fall upon you. When we stand in His glory, and we receive His freedom, we also become contagious to the "crowd" that surrounds us.

Today, I pray that God sets you free from any lies, hidden secrets, pains, problems, or anything that may be hiding behind the veil.

****

ASK YOURSELF:

What is God revealing to me today?
_____
_____
_____
_____
_____
_____

How do I see God working in my life today?
_____
_____
_____
_____
_____
_____

What can I do to bring a blessing to someone else?
_____
_____
_____
_____
_____
_____
_____

Journey Date 31_____

I was driving through my neighborhood one night and noticed the number of American flags that were waving in the wind. One of my neighbors has a spotlight that shines from the ground up to the flag. In the deep and darkness of the night that flag stood out above everything on the street.

As I saw this flag flying and moving so gently in the wind, I thought about how free it looked. Nothing holding it down, nothing stopping it from swaying back and forth. Freedom is an awesome thing. If you had to describe freedom to someone, how would you describe it? I saw freedom every time my son would put on his uniform when he was in the Army. I think of the freedom I have been given to choose where I live, who I married, how many children I could have, what I could name my children, but most of all the freedom to love the Lord my God with all of my heart, with all of my soul and all of my mind. You see it is a choice that God gives us. He gives the freedom to speak boldly about Him, to help others in need, to release us from our dark places by trusting in Him. Just like the flag that waves in the darkness, that is who HE is to us. He stands out above the rest of the world and His Spirit moves to and fro and gives us freedom.

"The Spirit of the Sovereign Lord is on me, because the Lord has anointed me to preach good news to the poor. He has sent me to bind up the brokenhearted, to proclaim FREEDOM for the captives and release them from the darkness to proclaim the year of the Lord's favor..." Isaiah 61: 1 & 2

Today, let His Spirit move to and fro in you and feel His freedom to heal any broken places in your heart.

****

ASK YOURSELF:

What is God revealing to me today?
_____
_____
_____
_____
_____
_____
_____
_____

How do I see God working in my life today?
_____
_____
_____
_____
_____
_____
_____
_____

What can I do to bring a blessing to someone else?
_____
_____
_____
_____
_____
_____
_____
_____

Journey Date 32_____

When my son was just over one year old, he pulled a Pyrex dish out from the cabinet and it fell a whole two inches to the floor, but in that instant the dish broke just like a dagger and sliced his little foot. We took him to the ER where the doctors proceeded to give him 10 stitches. The cut was approximately 1" long. I know there are people who have had several surgeries or "repairs" made, and they too have scars. Scars can be challenging and they usually carry an interesting story. Some scars are very visible. Some scars you can't see at all. Some scars grow in time, like my son's scar on his foot. The 1" scar on William's foot has now wrapped itself around the top, side and bottom of the foot. If it was measured, it would probably be about six inches long.

There are other scars though. These are the scars that most of us choose to hide. These can be the scars of pain, heartache, self-doubt and fear. Scars that came from a place in life, that it felt like a surgeon's knife was cutting deep into your heart and soul. I believe most of the scars are caused by unexpected "surgeries or repairs".

Our emotional scars are the same. Some of our scars are from so long ago, that the "length" of the scar is very visible. We don't expect to be hurt. We don't ask for pain. We didn't choose the divorce, the loss of a child, the car accident, the abusive parent, or the loss of a job. We don't look up to Heaven and ask God to "rain down pain"... but it happens. The problem is, we are told to hide "those kind of scars." We should just "deal with it". But these scars are just as real as the physical scars. Sometimes it is the physical scars that cause the "heart scars". We all have scars, of one kind or the other.

We are blessed though because our Savior received His scars before us. He knows the pain that we feel, because He felt it. He knows the humiliation that we feel, because he felt it. He knows the heartache we feel, because He felt it. Isaiah 53:4-5 is a prophetic word that tells us "*Surely He has borne our griefs and carried our sorrows...AND by HIS stripes (or wounds) we are healed!*" Jesus took the punishment so that we could release our "scars" to Him.

As strange as it sounds, Christ's scars, are beautiful scars. Without His scars we would not have a place to run to. Without His scars there could never be healing like He wants to give. Without His scars, we really would be nothing. Beautiful Scars... something for us to hold on to.

Today, my prayer for you, is that if you have open wounds, or scars that are still fresh and painful, trust the One who can be the ointment to make your scars beautiful too. Your beautiful scars may just be the salve, to the scars, of the person standing next to you. Be blessed and look at your scars with a whole new set of eyes.

✶✶

ASK YOURSELF:

What is God revealing to me today?

_____
_____
_____
_____
_____

How do I see God working in my life today?

_____
_____
_____
_____
_____

What can I do to bring a blessing to someone else?

_____
_____
_____
_____

Journey Date 33 _____

"Trust" - A small word with a whole lot of impact. If you know me, then you probably know that I have a soft heart for stray animals, or turtles crossing a street. Currently there are 2 cats that hang around our house whom I've creatively named Thomas (because he is a tom cat) and Mr. Gray, (because he is all gray). Of the two, Mr. Gray is definitely the "scaredy cat". When he first started coming to the house he would stay in the driveway, close to the car, and wait until I finished putting food in a bowl and then went inside the house. Now he actually comes to the door and sits and waits until someone brings him food, but he never let anyone pet him. As soon as you would reach down to touch him, he would run off. One day was different though. We came home and he was actually sleeping on the patio. We walked up and he started meowing for food. I brought him food and milk and sat down on the steps close to him. Normally he would run off, but this time he stayed. Gently I stroked his back, thinking surely he would leave. He just lifted his head and looked at me, like he was giving me approval and that he felt safe. He turned his head and kept lapping the milk, and I continued to gently pet his back. He looked quite happy. He finally got to a place where he trusts me.

Today, it seems difficult for us to trust. Who would you tell your deepest, darkest secret to and ***trust*** that it wouldn't get spread around the office or family or community? Are you like Mr. Gray, the "scaredy cat" who is leery of anyone and anything? Maybe you have been betrayed or hurt so deeply that the word "trust" just doesn't exist in your vocabulary. Or, maybe there is someone that you think of when you hear the word trust. One of my favorite and familiar passages is *Proverbs 3: 5 & 6... "Trust in the Lord with all your heart and lean not on your own understanding; in all your ways acknowledge Him and HE will make your paths straight."* You can trust the Lord with anything, with everything. You can tell Him your deepest, darkest secret and He will just draw you in closer to Him as a confirmation of His love.

Today, if you have a hard time trusting, take the first step, and reach out, and let the Lord love on you.

****

ASK YOURSELF:

What is God revealing to me today?

_____
_____
_____
_____
_____
_____
_____
_____

How do I see God working in my life today?

_____
_____
_____
_____
_____
_____
_____
_____

What can I do to bring a blessing to someone else?

_____
_____
_____
_____
_____
_____
_____

Journey Date 34_____

A friend of mine performed in the musical "The Wiz". For those of you who don't know, The Wiz is a modern day version of The Wizard of Oz. We all know the story… Dorothy encounters the Scarecrow, the Tin Man, and the Lion. All of them were searching for something. They traveled together, longing for the one "thing" that would fulfill their greatest desire. They followed their instructions and they traveled down the Yellow Brick Road. Can you hear the song now… "Follow the yellow brick road, follow the yellow brick road, follow, follow, follow, follow, follow the yellow brick road…". They knew where to go and what road to take, but, along the way they encountered several obstacles. I am sure they were afraid and at times I believe they had doubts about whether or not they were going to make it to their destination to get that one thing. Of course, the Lion got his courage, the Tin Man got his heart, the Scarecrow got his brains, and eventually Dorothy got to go home. The common thread though is that they were all longing for something that was missing.

Aren't we the same way today? We are longing for that one thing that seems to be missing. That one thing that we think is our greatest desire, and once we have it, then life will be peaceful and complete. I remember thinking that "if only I could have my first new car, then everything would be perfect. At the young age of 20, I got the new car. I had it for six months and then it was totaled in an accident. My one thing was gone instantly. For some people it may be the thought of a getting a house, or maybe a new job, or even any job if you are unemployed. For some it may be "the perfect relationship with that perfect person". Of course we find out week, months and years later that no one is perfect.

Is there that one thing that you feel is missing in your life? I have found that even when I obtain those "one things" that "something" still felt empty. Then I discovered what the "one thing" was… Jesus. He tells us in John 14:27 – *"Peace I leave with you; MY peace I give you. I do not give as the world gives. Do not let your hearts be troubled and do not be afraid."* Don't misunderstand what I am saying, it is okay to search for those things that are deep within your heart, but when you search for them with Christ the search becomes much easier.

Today, I pray that our Lord will pour out peace and clear direction, and that when travel down your yellow brick road you will know He is near.

****

ASK YOURSELF:

What is God revealing to me today?

_____
_____
_____
_____
_____
_____
_____
_____

How do I see God working in my life today?

_____
_____
_____
_____
_____
_____
_____
_____

What can I do to bring a blessing to someone else?

_____
_____
_____
_____
_____
_____

Journey Date 35_____

I was meditating on the word GUIDANCE, and I kept seeing "dance" at the end of the word. My first thought of dancing would be to dance with a partner. What would happen if two people try to lead? Nothing would feel right. The movement doesn't flow with the music, and everything is quite uncomfortable and jerky. How can both people be the leader, demanding that their way is the right way to move. Someone has to be willing to follow. If you are like me, sometimes it is really hard to follow. Maybe it's a lot of times that I want to be in control. But, when dancing, if one person realizes and lets the other lead, both bodies begin to flow with the music. One gives gentle clues, perhaps with a nudge to the back or by pressing lightly in one direction or another. It's as if two become one body, moving beautifully. The dance takes surrender, willingness, and attentiveness from one person and gentle guidance and skill from the other. I read some time ago, that doing God's will is a lot like dancing.

Looking back at the word GUIDANCE, I saw "G," and I thought of God, followed by "u" and "i." "God, "u" and "i" dance."! God, you, and I dance. This statement is what guidance means to me. I should be willing to trust that I would get guidance about my life from God. When I surrender and have willingness to let Him guide, amazing things take place. Sometimes He gives very clear guidance and direction through friends or family. At other times His guidance seems to be very quiet, and I have to search for the direction. But, He always gives it if I ask for it. Don't misunderstand what I am saying… God gives guidance in many types of ways. We can't just sit and wait for the door to physically open and hear God's voice telling us "Go get in your car and get groceries for your home." He wants to guide us by His truths and teachings. Psalms 25: 4-5 says it like this… *"Show me Your ways oh Lord, teach me Your paths; guide me in Your truth and teach me, for You are God my Savior, and my hope is in you all day long."* God's dance in life is just that… dancing in His ways, His truth, His paths… and He will give us hope all the days of our lives.

Today will you "dance" with the Lord and enjoy His presence? He wants to dance with you.

✲✲✲

ASK YOURSELF:

What is God revealing to me today?

_____
_____
_____
_____
_____
_____
_____
_____

How do I see God working in my life today?

_____
_____
_____
_____
_____
_____
_____
_____

What can I do to bring a blessing to someone else?

_____
_____
_____
_____
_____
_____

Journey Date 36_____

Sitting here my mind seems to draw a blank. How unusual that seems to be. Normally my mind is filled with so many things…children, husband, work, friends, God, weather, dinner, laundry, and the list goes on. But today, is just a little different. It's as if God has given my mind a reprieve… "a time out" you might say. As wonderful as that may seem to most of us, there seems to be an underlying feeling of guilt. A guilt that makes me think that I should be "doing something". There are so many things that need to be done, why is there a "blank"? Why is there stillness? Why should I get a "time out"? Why is there quiet, when it appears that the rest of the world around me is in turmoil? Do I really deserve the stillness and time of quiet? Carpe' Diem is where my heart and soul want to be… seizing every moment of life. How can I seize a "blank"? Then all of sudden, a still small voice sounds in my mind… "yes, you deserve to rest, even in these times of turmoil." There it was, the idea that you can seize even the quiet moments in their fullest.

It seems that we hurry and rush and plan and run here and there, and it's difficult to stop and seize the quiet moments. Are you like me, with a sense of feeling guilt if you do stop? Possibly it isn't the stopping of the body that is difficult, but it's the stopping of the mind. Does it race everywhere, wondering, worrying, and wanting, without shutting off? You know, when you lay down at night and it just seems that the brain just won't turn off? I am learning that it really is okay to stop and be "blank" for a moment. Psalm 46:10 says it simply, ***"Be still*** *and know that I am God…"*

Pretty simple thought… be still, Be Still, BE STILL… just be still and let the world of worries fall away for a moment, and know that God is sitting right there in the stillness with you. It really is okay.

Today, I hope that as your day goes flying by, and life seems to be rushing past, that for just a moment, you will have that "time out". Seize the stillness and bask in the quiet.

****

ASK YOURSELF:

What is God revealing to me today?
_____
_____
_____
_____
_____
_____
_____
_____

How do I see God working in my life today?
_____
_____
_____
_____
_____
_____
_____
_____

What can I do to bring a blessing to someone else?
_____
_____
_____
_____
_____
_____
_____

Journey Date 37_____

Have you ever thought about getting ready for the day, all of the things that you do? I know that I actually "prepare" myself to start the day. I get out of bed, turn on the Keurig, take a shower, go make myself a cup of hot tea, I brush my teeth, dry my hair, get dressed for the day, take my vitamins and then begin to think about what the day holds. If I didn't prepare myself, you probably wouldn't want to be near me. So I do these things each day to bring a freshness for myself in preparing for the new day.

You know it is the same way with our Father and our relationship with Him. He desires to prepare each day for us. He wants us to look for the new adventures of the day. He wants to give us His strength and His Spirit so that we can walk throughout the day in peace and full of joy.

Ephesians 3:16 says, *"I ask the Father in His great glory to give you the power to be strong inwardly through HIS spirit."* I read this and believe that God desires to prepare you for the day and give you His blessings and power through Him. All you have to do is ask and He would love to cover you with these wonderful gifts.

Today, I hope today you know how special you are to Him. You are His and He is yours Be refreshed in peace and joy!

****

ASK YOURSELF:

What is God revealing to me today?
_____
_____
_____
_____
_____
_____
_____
_____

How do I see God working in my life today?
_____
_____
_____
_____
_____
_____
_____
_____

What can I do to bring a blessing to someone else?
_____
_____
_____
_____
_____
_____
_____
_____

Journey Date 38_____

Once again, while driving to work, on a wet and rainy road, it seemed that the curves and bumps were more noticeable. I took notice of the pot holes and the part of the road that was old and beginning to have crevices and cracks. I thought maybe I was on a roller coaster ride, not missing any of the bumpy places and sliding through a couple of slick spots. Then, came a place where the road was brand new. No cracks, no pot holes, no bumps, just flat, straight and easy to cross. The roller coaster ride was coming to a calm and peaceful part of the track. The new road ended and the ride started all over again.

Isn't this what our life is about? Do you ever feel like your life is like that road? Bumpy, slippery, with cracks and crevices and potholes through it? God desires to keep us safe on our road of life. In Psalms 91 we are told, *"Those who go to God Most High for safety will be protected by the Almighty."*

How often do we go to Him for that safety? Or do we try to solve all of our problems and issues in life, our way. By ourselves. He is waiting to smooth out the "rough roads" of life, by protecting, by bringing peace and joy and by loving you.

Today, I encourage you to focus on the part of your life that is like the new road and know that you are in the protection of His mighty hands.

****

ASK YOURSELF:

What is God revealing to me today?
_____
_____
_____
_____
_____
_____
_____

How do I see God working in my life today?
_____
_____
_____
_____
_____
_____
_____

What can I do to bring a blessing to someone else?
_____
_____
_____
_____
_____
_____
_____

Journey Date 39_____

Have you ever wondered about the Spirit of God and where it really is? His spirit is everywhere - can you see it? When was the last time you took a walk through the woods, or drove to the top of a mountain, or walked along a shoreline?

In those places there always seems to be silence, or a breeze blowing, or branches clapping together. Something in those places that seem so much greater than yourself. Awe and wonder strike a "heart chord", and you wish you could touch it. But what about in the tears of your husband or the tears of your wife, in the smile of a little child, in the playfulness of a puppy or a kitten. His Presence is in the rain that falls down and sun that shines. It is in the heart of the person that stands next to you. Just look around you, and you will see His Spirit.

David asks the question in Psalm 139 *"where can I go from your Spirit? Where can I flee from Your Presence?"* We are given the opportunity to see Him in all places, because he does not hide from us. He is everywhere.

Today, look in the eyes of someone you love and then look into your own eyes, and you will see Him there. I see Him daily, I hope you will too.

****

ASK YOURSELF:

What is God revealing to me today?

_____
_____
_____
_____
_____
_____
_____
_____

How do I see God working in my life today?

_____
_____
_____
_____
_____
_____
_____
_____
_____

What can I do to bring a blessing to someone else?

_____
_____
_____
_____
_____
_____
_____
_____

Journey Date 40_____

Imagine yourself in a vast place that is so immense and full of life... then all of a sudden the lights go out and it is pitch black. You are there, feeling totally alone, in the darkness, not one glimmer of light around you. You can't see anything or anyone. You can't hear anything or anyone. You wonder "how long will I have to stay here?"

And out of the darkness, in the far away corner there is a tiny glimmer, almost like a match being lit, and yours eyes become completely focused on that tiny light. You walk toward it, thinking if you do, it will lead you out of the darkness. The closer you get the brighter the light gets. You become more focused, searching for the "escape door". You just want out of the darkness. You continue to walk toward the match light. It becomes more like a flashlight, then like a beacon light... you stay completely focused... when you reach the light it engulfs you and you stand covered in light and you can see the door, you can see the pathway to the "outside".

You forget the dark that you were standing in and you go forward. Psalm 18:16-19 says it this way *"He reached from on high and took hold of me; He drew me out of deep waters. He rescued me from my powerful enemy, from my foes, who were too strong for me. They comfort me in the day of my disaster, but the Lord was my support. He brought me out into a spacious place; He rescued me because He delighted in me."*

Today, if you are standing in a dark place whether it is physical, emotional, mental or financial, HE is holding up the match to guide you. Focus on the match...you will be bathed in His light.

****

ASK YOURSELF:

What is God revealing to me today?

_____
_____
_____
_____
_____
_____
_____
_____

How do I see God working in my life today?

_____
_____
_____
_____
_____
_____
_____
_____
_____

What can I do to bring a blessing to someone else?

_____
_____
_____
_____
_____
_____
_____
_____

Journey Date 41_____

We have two cats. One of the cats was a real "fraidy" cat. Bill has won her heart over and has brought her out of her shell. How? One simple word … "treats". We found these chewy, soft, chicken flavored cat treats that Chicago Girl loves. Bill and The Girl have a routine every day, where she knows she is going to get some treats. Even better yet, he has trained her to understand the word "treats". All he has to do is say "TREATS" and she comes running. She sits on the floor in front of him, kind of like a dog, waiting for her treats. She knows she won't get any though, until she jumps up on the armrest of the couch and gives Bill a little nudge. But she knows if she does these things, she is going to get a chewy morsel of chicken flavored delights.

Recently though, in her devouring of treats, she left some of the crumbs behind, sitting on the arm rest. In the meantime, Bill got himself an evening snack of cookies and milk, and set the cookies on the armrest while he was getting comfortable. Not knowing that The Girl had left some of her tasty morsels behind. He picked up his cookies and began to eat them. He noticed that there were some "crumbs" left on the armrest, and picked them up and threw them in his mouth. No sense in wasting good cookie crumbs. Quickly he realized that in the midst of the cookie crumbs was a leftover cat treat. Ugh! How awful was that! The cat treat actually looked like a small morsel of the cookie. But, oh, it did NOT taste like a yummy cookie at all.

This was a perfect example though of what we fall prey to. How many times do we see something that we think we must have and we buy it, only to feel guilty later. Or possibly that we are tempted to do something that we know will be harmful in the long run, but our mind convinces us that "it" won't be that bad if we only do "it" once. Or, we long to be in a relationship with someone so desperately that we settle for a companion who brings more pain than love. The bottom line on all of these things is deception. Just like the little cat treat, it was hiding itself amongst the yummy cookie crumbs. Bill couldn't even tell the difference, but as soon as he tasted it, he knew it was bad.

It is so easy to be deceived by money, power and relationships. Yet, we have a wonderful Savior who will protect us from the deception when we ask Him to. Several times Christ tells us, "do not be deceived" … "follow me and you will receive your reward in Heaven." Maybe you are on a road that just doesn't feel right, and you wonder why. Maybe you are considering a turn in your life that doesn't fit what you know is true. Ask our Lord to show you the truth, and to make the path clear and without deception.

Today, truth awaits each and every one of us. It's God's promise to us. His truth will set us free, and free indeed we will be.

****

ASK YOURSELF:

What is God revealing to me today?

_____
_____
_____
_____
_____

How do I see God working in my life today?

_____
_____
_____
_____
_____

What can I do to bring a blessing to someone else?

_____
_____
_____
_____
_____

Journey Date 42_____

When was the last time that you went to an art gallery? My children are very creative and have a great ability to capture their love of life in their talents of drawing, painting and photography, and have had several pieces of their work entered into art contests and made it to the gallery.

Every time I go and look at the many different aspects of art I am fascinated at how each piece is so individual. Each person that created their work, took time, effort and exactness to make their masterpiece to look exactly like it looks. Every brush stroke is important, until the final one is placed, and the artist signs their name to the work. Every pencil line on the drawing, every piece of paper placed on the mache', and the countless numbers of photographs until the perfect one is taken. Every piece has a beginning and an end, and along the way there are touch ups and re-dos and then all of sudden, there it is... the finished product!
Perfection at the end!

Do you know that you are the same way? Every day is a new stroke of the brush by God. He is preparing you for the perfection that HE sees in you. Philippians 1:6 tells us, *"He who began a good work in you, will see it to completion until the day of Jesus Christ."* You see, God started his good work with you the day you were being formed in your mother's womb, and each day He places one more pencil line, one more brush stroke, one more polishing of the silver until your day of completion, which will be when we are facing Christ. We are all in the place of being formed for the perfection of Him. That's it. Nothing more, nothing less, BUT, we are being placed here on earth by Him to share about HIS perfection, not ours.

Today you may not be perfect, but you are being painted on. What a beautiful picture God is painting as HE paints you! He has signed His name on you because YOU are His masterpiece!

****

ASK YOURSELF:

What is God revealing to me today?

_____
_____
_____
_____
_____
_____
_____
_____

How do I see God working in my life today?

_____
_____
_____
_____
_____
_____
_____
_____

What can I do to bring a blessing to someone else?

_____
_____
_____
_____
_____
_____
_____

Journey Date 43_____

Have you ever woken up with that "starving" hungry feeling? You know, the one where your stomach is growling so loud that you think it will wake everyone up in the house. That feeling of, "if I don't get something to eat or drink quickly, I may just pass out." Have you ever had that feeling? You are so hungry you just HAVE to have something to fill that emptiness in your belly or there may be some major consequences to the pantry?

We are the same way with our emotions and our heart. There are times we have that empty hungry feeling in our soul and we are longing for something to fill it. Something that will give us complete satisfaction. Longing for a relationship that will never run dry, but is always fulfilling. Have you ever had that feeling? Are you longing for the empty space in your heart to be filled? That something is Jesus.

John 6:35 says, *"I am the bread of life. He who comes to ME will never go hungry and he who believes in ME will never be thirsty. "*

Today are you feeling hungry or thirsty, or do you have that "empty place" inside of you? Call out the name above all names... and He will satisfy you to never feel that emptiness again.

****

ASK YOURSELF:

What is God revealing to me today?
_____
_____
_____
_____
_____
_____
_____
_____

How do I see God working in my life today?
_____
_____
_____
_____
_____
_____
_____
_____
_____

What can I do to bring a blessing to someone else?
_____
_____
_____
_____
_____
_____
_____
_____

Journey Date 44_____

Have you ever been on a train ride? Our family took a train ride several years ago through the Colorado mountains. There were parts of the ride that the scenery was so breath taking, that you knew God was standing beside you. Then there were the tunnels. As we would approach the tunnel, I would wonder how long was the tunnel, how long would it be dark, when would we reach the other side? I always knew that there would be light at the end of the tunnel, I just didn't know when I would see it. It seemed like such an uneasy feeling to be in the unending beauty of the Colorado mountains, but couldn't see it.

 Our lives are the same way. You may be approaching a tunnel or maybe you have been in the tunnel for a while and you are just waiting to see the breaking light and the beauty of God. Or, you may be standing on the other side of the tunnel, breathing in the freshness of God... wherever you are, I want to remind you of what God tells us in Isaiah. Read the words below and put your name in the blank and know that He will never leave you or forsake you.

*"Fear not _____, I have redeemed you; I the Lord have called you by your name; you are Mine. When you pass through the waters, I will be with you; and through the rivers, they shall not overflow you. When you walk through the fire, you will not be burned and the flame will not scorch you. _____,
you are Mine!"* - Isaiah 43: 1 & 2

Today, remember that our Savior is right beside you in the darkness and will be with you through the "tunnel" of life.

****

ASK YOURSELF:

What is God revealing to me today?
_____
_____
_____
_____
_____
_____
_____
_____

How do I see God working in my life today?
_____
_____
_____
_____
_____
_____
_____
_____

What can I do to bring a blessing to someone else?
_____
_____
_____
_____
_____
_____
_____
_____

Journey Date 45_____

My dog, Charlie, is getting old. He is coming up on 12 years now. You know that proverbial statement, "Do you want to go outside" always gets a dog up and running. Well, lately it doesn't even move him off of the couch (yes, he does get on our couch). We thought maybe was losing interest in going outside as often, and just enjoyed resting on the couch or laying on the floor, or just relaxing as an older dog will do. But we realized that he had become hard of hearing. If we get really close to him and speak very loud, he perks up out of his restful place and trots over to the door. I have watched him over time and see how much he ignores (because he can't hear) all of the outside noises. Nothing bothers him anymore. He just rests.

I thought about this and realized we can do the same thing. Not that we want to be hard of hearing, but that we can rest in our Lord. When we stop the "outside noises" (possibly the voice of our greatest enemy) and listen to the voice of our Lord we can rest in our circumstances and know that HE will take care of us. *Psalm 91:1 and Matthew 11:28 tell us, "He who dwells in the shelter of the Most High will REST in the Shadow of the Almighty"* and Jesus says, *"Come to ME all who are weary and burdened and I will give you REST."*

My dear friends and family, no matter what you are going through, I pray that you will close your ears for just a moment to the noise that may be confusing or painful and REST in the calming words of our Lord.

Today, rest on the couch, lay on the floor, or just sit at your desk and let HIM bathe you in His shelter.

****

ASK YOURSELF:

What is God revealing to me today?

_____
_____
_____
_____
_____
_____
_____
_____

How do I see God working in my life today?

_____
_____
_____
_____
_____
_____
_____
_____

What can I do to bring a blessing to someone else?

_____
_____
_____
_____
_____
_____
_____

Journey Date 46_____

Today it seems that the word "life" means "to hurry". How many times in a day do you hurry to get all of your chores done? How many times do you tell your children or your co-workers that we need to "hurry up and get this done because we have so many other things to do". How many meetings, soccer games, rehearsals, and deadlines do we all have on our platter each day?

Some days the platter seems like it is so full that we just want to stop and yell "NO MORE!" Even when we think we are accomplishing the things that need to be done, and start peeling the pieces off of the platter, more gets added and the platter seems to never be empty. Then the toppings on the platter become piled with stress, then a little anxiety is poured on, and then worry and depression may become the final topping.

David tells us in the Psalms that we need to be still and know that God is our refuge and strength. *"God is our refuge and strength, an ever-present help in trouble. Therefore we will not fear..." Psalms 46:1.* God tells us in Psalm 46:10 - *"Be STILL and know that I AM GOD!"*

Today as your "life" continues to bring new challenges, I encourage that to take the time to stop and be still. Turn off the TV, turn off the Smartphone or computer, and if you can, go into your closet and rest in Him. Be still and know that HE is God. HE is your refuge.

****

ASK YOURSELF:

What is God revealing to me today?
_____
_____
_____
_____
_____
_____
_____
_____

How do I see God working in my life today?
_____
_____
_____
_____
_____
_____
_____
_____

What can I do to bring a blessing to someone else?
_____
_____
_____
_____
_____
_____
_____
_____

Journey Date 47_____

Every day I drive to and from work I pass by a landfill. I have noticed in the hot afternoons that there is usually a flock of buzzards flying in the sky over this lovely piece of land. As we all know, buzzards or vultures as you may call them, look for the dying "specimen". They perch for hours watching and waiting for their prey to take its last breath, and then they go in for the devouring. As I have taken notice of these creatures I find that they are very persistent. They fly and they watch, and they fly and they watch, never taking their eyes off of their victim. When their prey finally gives in to death, they go in and destroy what is left of the dying animal and the buzzards have their feast. Have you ever thought if only the animal would run for safety or go and hide somewhere the buzzards could not get to it?

You may feel like you are in a "landfill" and it seems that death is all around you, and the "buzzards" are flying over your head waiting for you to fall. I tell you today, that Jesus says *"I AM the bread of life. He who comes to Me will never be hungry and he who believes in Me will never be thirsty."* He tells us, *"The thief comes only to steal and kill and destroy; but I have come that you may have life and have it to the fullest."* (John 6:35 and John 10:10)

If you are feeling like the specimen and the buzzards are watching remember that God is watching you too. He is wanting you to run to Him and hide in Him so that He may give you life and take care of you. He does not want your enemy to devour you, but He wants to give you a fresh drink.

Today, I pray that you will feel His comfort all around you, and believe that He is covering you with arms of peace.

✻✻

ASK YOURSELF:

What is God revealing to me today?

_____
_____
_____
_____
_____
_____
_____
_____
_____

How do I see God working in my life today?

_____
_____
_____
_____
_____
_____
_____
_____
_____

What can I do to bring a blessing to someone else?

_____
_____
_____
_____
_____
_____
_____
_____

Journey Date 48_____

My husband and I owned three vehicles. One of them was born in 1995 and two were born in 1996. Needless to say they are all having some "issues" and in need of "road repair". My father graciously let us borrow his 1995 Cadillac Sedan Deville, while he had been on vacation. He told us that the car needed an oil change, and if we wouldn't mind, could we get it done. So my husband took the car to our usual place. He drove up and a new fellow popped the hood and just stood there in amazement. He came in and looked at my husband and just said "WOW man - I don't think I've ever seen a car so clean". Now I know my father, he takes great care of his vehicles. He "cleans" the engine with that "engine degreaser cleaner stuff". And he changes the oil regularly and rotates the tires and does all the things that it takes to keep the car running in good shape. I can remember him always telling me that however you care for your vehicle, is how it will return its use.

As goofy as it sounds, we are like my dad's Cadillac. If we ask our Father in Heaven to keep us clean and "change our oil" and "rotate our tires" He will give us a "clean heart". I love what Psalm 51 says: *"Create in me a clean heart, O God and renew a steadfast spirit within me. Do not cast me from Your Presence or take Your Holy Spirit from me. Restore to me the joy of Your salvation and grant me a willing spirit to sustain me."* Psalm 51: 10-12

"Create In Me A Clean Heart" is one of my favorite songs to sing. I hope that you will sing these words to your Father and let Him give you and oil change today.

Today, let Him clean and renew you with His Holy Spirit and restore your joy.

****

ASK YOURSELF:

What is God revealing to me today?

_____
_____
_____
_____
_____
_____
_____

How do I see God working in my life today?

_____
_____
_____
_____
_____
_____
_____

What can I do to bring a blessing to someone else?

_____
_____
_____
_____
_____
_____
_____

Journey Date 49_____

I have a friend who shared a great story with me, and I would like to pass on to you. She has a little boy, who just turned 6. As a younger boy his parents had given him a children's Bible. You know, the ones with the short abbreviated stories and very colorful pictures. It was a beginning place for him to learn to know who God and Jesus were. My friend tells me that he loved his Bible and carried it proudly. As he has reached this "old age" of 6, the little boy was given a "Big" Bible. She said his eyes got huge and was so excited to get a "big person's" Bible. He apparently took the Bible to his room and glanced through the new crisp pages and began reading at Genesis 1. Then he came out to talk to his mom and said with such innocence "mommy, do I have to read this whole thing in one night?"

What an amazing desire to learn more and search for God at such a young age.

If we could only be like this little boy. Hungering and thirsting to want to know the "whole" story of Lord. Jesus tells us to come him as little children, just trusting and loving and desiring. *"Let the little children come to Me, and do not hinder them, for the Kingdom of God belongs to such as these. I tell you the truth, anyone who will not receive the Kingdom of God like a little child will never enter it."* - Matthew 19:14, Mark 10:14, Luke 18:16.

Today let your hunger and thirst be as my friends' little boy, carrying God's word proudly with you, longing to know the whole story of a Savior who died, so we could live.

****

ASK YOURSELF:

What is God revealing to me today?
_____
_____
_____
_____
_____
_____
_____
_____

How do I see God working in my life today?
_____
_____
_____
_____
_____
_____
_____
_____
_____

What can I do to bring a blessing to someone else?
_____
_____
_____
_____
_____
_____
_____
_____

Journey Date 50_____

Some time ago, my family added a new addition to it. No I am not a grandmother, NOR have I had more children... but we do have a gray and white tiger stripped kitten. My daughter Katy and I came up with the name "Chicago Girl" (that is another story in itself). If you have ever had a kitten or a puppy you will understand the passion for playfulness that is born within them. Then on the other hand, they are still trying to figure out how to stay "protected" from the "big bad uglies" out there (like our German Sheperd Charlie) and where to go for rest and feel safe. Chicago Girl has found her resting place... it is in my daughter Katy. She will run for Katy's room when she feels afraid and Katy will pick her up and pet her and hold her close and talk to her calmly. Then Chicago girl will curl up around Katy's neck or on Katy's stomach and just lay and rest and fall sound asleep. All of the cares in the world could be crashing down around her, but Chicago Girl knows that she is safe in Katy's presence.

We are like Chicago Girl. Life hands us many circumstances that seem to keep us running. Some of them are good circumstance, and many of them are difficult. Your life may be full of the "big bad uglies", it may be so full that you feel there is no place to run and feel protected and at rest.

Jesus is your resting place. He is the one you can run to, and hide in His presence. He will let you curl up next to Him and He will hold you close and bring you comfort. Jesus tells us in Matthew, *"Come to ME, all you who are weary and heavy burdened, and I will give you rest. Take MY yoke upon you and learn from Me, for I am gentle and humble in heart, and you will find rest for your souls. For My yoke is easy and my burden is light".:* - Matthew 11:28-29

Today run to Him and leap in His arms and rest. We all need to rest. My prayer for you is that you will know His presence is there with you, bringing you rest and peaceful moments.

✳✳

ASK YOURSELF:

What is God revealing to me today?

How do I see God working in my life today?

What can I do to bring a blessing to someone else?

Journey Date 51_____

Last night I took our kitten, Chicago Girl, to get her first set of shots. As I was putting her in the cat carrier, she thought it was fun... at first. Then she realized I was locking the door and carrying her outside. She scrambled around in the carrier for a minute or so and then we took off in the truck. I could tell by her meowing and pacing back and forth in the carrier that she wasn't quite sure of what was going on. Each time she meowed, I would talk to her. I would speak in a soft voice and tell her "it's okay, we will be there soon". I would call out her name "Chicago Girl - sweet kitty - it's okay, I am here for you." She knew my voice which seemed to give her comfort for just the moments she could hear it, but then she would cry again.

Our drive was about 10 minutes to the vet, but to her, it must have seemed like hours. When we arrived at our destination, I took her in the carrier and gave her to the veterinarian. She got her shots and we went back to the truck. I opened the cage and she calmly walked out and crawled in my lap. She knew she had to trust me to get her back home safely. I continued to talk to her and hold her close and then opened the door of the carrier. Willingly she went back inside and laid down. It was as if she knew she had to trust me and not her own instincts.

Proverbs 3:5-6 tells us to do same thing with our lives and God. *"Trust in the Lord with ALL your heart and lean not on your own understanding, in ALL your ways acknowledge Him and He shall direct your paths."* God knows what place you are in. He knows the "cat carrier" of your life and hears you calling out to Him. He knows the pains, the hurts, the heartaches, the trials. He knows the joy, the laughter and the tears that you cry.

Today know His Presence is in your path, and even for a moment, tell Him you trust Him with your life and your circumstances and HE will take care of you.

✳✳

ASK YOURSELF:

What is God revealing to me today?

_____
_____
_____
_____
_____
_____
_____
_____

How do I see God working in my life today?

_____
_____
_____
_____
_____
_____
_____
_____

What can I do to bring a blessing to someone else?

_____
_____
_____
_____
_____
_____
_____
_____

Journey Date 52_____

Have you ever left your car running for a long period of time, parked in one spot? My son parked our GEO Tracker at school one rainy day and he proceeded to take the key out of the ignition and head for class. At 2:04 PM he takes his afternoon trip back to the car, ready to unlock the door, and he noticed that his car keys were missing. As the rain kept coming down, he realized the car was running. His keychain snaps apart, and he thought he taken the entire set, but the car key was still in the ignition and the car was never turned off. It sat in one place, for almost six hours, running idly, but not moving. Now fortunately it was still sitting in the same place. (I call that a miracle, even if it is a 1995 GEO Tracker). I have thought about this incident; gas being pumped into the engine, the engine NEVER being turned off, and yet the car didn't go anywhere. Obviously it didn't go anywhere because there wasn't a driver. No one to steer the wheel or to shift the gears. No one to give the car direction.

There are times that I feel like I am that car in my realationship with God. My engine continues to run, sometimes a million miles an hour, but I don't get anywhere. I don't let God put me in gear or turn the steering wheel. I try to do it myself or I just park myself in my self-pity or in my difficult circumstances and I use up all of the fuel. One of God's greatest promises is found in Jeremiah 29. Let me write it out here:

"For I know the plans I have for you", <u>DECLARES the Lord</u>, *"plans to prosper you and not to harm you, plans to give you hope and a future. Then you will call upon ME and come and pray to Me, and I WILL listen to you."* - Jeremiah 29: 11 & 12

You see God has such great plans for you, and for me, if we will just let Him drive our life. It isn't just that he "says" He has a plan for us... He DECLARES IT! Isn't that exciting?! I hope today that He will steer your "vehicle" and you will know that He is driving you in the right direction.

Today, may the greatest driver of all, be your guide.

****

ASK YOURSELF:

What is God revealing to me today?

_____
_____
_____
_____
_____
_____
_____
_____

How do I see God working in my life today?

_____
_____
_____
_____
_____
_____
_____
_____

What can I do to bring a blessing to someone else?

_____
_____
_____
_____
_____
_____
_____

Journey Date 53_____

There is so much on my mind today that I just can't seem to focus on one thing. There are many people in my life who are dealing with different heartaches, pains and sufferings. Several friends of mine are dealing with cancer, brain cancer, lung cancer and breast cancer. I have a friend who is struggling in their marriage. Another friend longs for communication with their children. Yet another friend desires to have a baby. My sister had some negative test results on her pap smear, twice, as well as undergoing long treatment of a bladder disease. Another friend's 7 year old daughter is in the process of having major dental surgery and having her teeth extracted. Many others are recovering from the loss of a dear loved one and others are suffering from the loss of their financial income. Another of my friends wakes up every day wondering what else can happen to their physical health, and others who just want to wake up and breathe a breath of fresh air to get them through their depression.

As I sat and prayed and thought about the many people whom I love, who God has put in my path, (you), I thought there is no way that I can help or do anything to give them comfort or peace. Clearly He showed me, "you are right, you can't, but "I - GOD" can!" Words from our Savior tell us ....

"Peace I leave with you, MY peace I give to you, not as the world gives do I give to you. Let not your heart be troubled, neither let it be afraid." - John 14:27

Today, you may recognize yourself in one of these places, or several of these places. If you are reading these words, I have prayed for you. I promise you that Jesus will give you the peace that you long for. As you read these words I hope that you feel His presence and know HIS peace is blanketing you now.

✳✳

ASK YOURSELF:

What is God revealing to me today?
_____
_____
_____
_____
_____
_____
_____
_____

How do I see God working in my life today?
_____
_____
_____
_____
_____
_____
_____
_____

What can I do to bring a blessing to someone else?
_____
_____
_____
_____
_____
_____
_____
_____

Journey Date 54_____

I remember growing up and hearing the saying, "Absence makes the heart grow fonder." I wasn't too sure of what that meant until I got older. You know what that message really means, right?... "Leave now honey, because you are driving me crazy, and I need some time alone - but don't be gone too long, because I will miss you soon." In years past my husband traveled quite a bit. He would be gone two or three weeks at a time and then return for a weekend and then depart again. As a family, we began to get use to his schedule and "know" that he would return. But Charlie, our German Shepherd, wasn't always so sure of that. No matter if Bill was gone one day or one month, Charlie would ALWAYS great him with a hug and a smile that only a dog could give (literally the dog would get up on the bed and put his paws on Bills' shoulders and lay his head on on Bills' chest).

I have thought about this saying lately and realized it is not a very good statement when you want a relationship to grow. I think time apart helps me to understand how much I desire to have a "daily" relationship with my husband, not just the weekends. Charlie doesn't know any different, he just knows that he is to "love" on Bill every time Bill walks through the door.

We should be like Charlie with our relationship with God. God so desires for us to have that "daily' relationship with Him. He doesn't want to wait for weekends when "we" walk through "His" doors. He wants us to develop that relationship every single day and not wait to be absent from Him to have a closer relationship. Jesus is asked what the greatest commandment is. His response is found in Mark 12:30 – *"Love the Lord your God, with all of your heart, with all of your soul and with all of your mind, and all of your strength."*

Today, no matter where you are with God, tell Him how much you love Him and let Him walk into the door of your heart.

****

ASK YOURSELF:

What is God revealing to me today?

_____
_____
_____
_____
_____
_____
_____
_____

How do I see God working in my life today?

_____
_____
_____
_____
_____
_____
_____
_____

What can I do to bring a blessing to someone else?

_____
_____
_____
_____
_____
_____
_____
_____

Journey Date 55_____

Yesterday I was at the gym working out. I always take my own music so that I can listen to I want to. There I was riding on the bike, listening to the album that I chose, and it seemed that my music was getting softer, or the music in the gym was getting louder. I turned up my music to "drown out" the music at the gym. Then there were people who got on other machines that were near me. One was making a really loud noise as they walked on the treadmill. The other person was talking to someone next to them and because the music was so loud in the gym, they were talking loud. So, I turned up MY music again, just a little bit louder to try and "drown out" more noise. I kept peddling, trying to focus on the music that was now seemingly blaring in my ears... then some fellows decided to play basketball on the courts, so now I could hear the thumping of the basketball and the whopping and yelling on the courts. I finally decided to just give in and turn the music up as loud as it could go – which may have caused some deafness, but I wanted to focus on MY music and not everything else around me.

Our lives are much like this. So many things creep into our lives that take over the focus of our lives. Surely you know what I mean. First off, our jobs – how much attention does it get? Then our family, then our church, then our friends, then our pets, then comes illnesses along the way, or disaster's, or death, or even the fun events in our life. We must always remember that God is our first focus in ALL of these things.

God tells us in Isaiah 55: 3 - *"Listen carefully to ME, and eat what is good. And let your soul delight itself in abundance. Incline your ear, and come to ME. Hear, and your soul shall live. And I WILL make an everlasting covenant with you."*

Isn't that awesome! All we have to do is listen with our ears and come near to God and He has promised us an everlasting covenant with Him. I don't know what "things" you are trying to "drown out", so stop for just a moment, even if it is right now, and spend 30 seconds just in silence, listening to God. It may be hard for you to stop... but I urge you to take a moment for yourself and try it.

Today may God bless you and may you see that He makes Himself real in a special way.

****

ASK YOURSELF:

What is God revealing to me today?

_____
_____
_____
_____
_____
_____
_____

How do I see God working in my life today?

_____
_____
_____
_____
_____
_____
_____
_____
_____

What can I do to bring a blessing to someone else?

_____
_____
_____
_____
_____
_____
_____

Journey Date 56_____

One Sunday morning I decided to attend the "early, early" service at church. I left the house at 8:00 am and drove about 1 mile and it seemed as though I was driving into a cloud. As I kept driving, I realized I really was driving in a cloud. It was the strangest feeling. The sky was dull yellow and I could sense the sun was really trying to creep through the clouds, but the further I drove, the denser the cloud became. In order to get to my church I had to drive down two lane, bumpy, curvy country roads. Here it was – the sky was "suppose" to be light, but it wasn't, the roads are usually clear, but they weren't, using headlights on the car is not usually necessary, but it was. The best word's that comes to my mind about what was going on around me is "eerie uneasiness". I don't even know if those words go together, but that is how I felt while driving. I couldn't see five feet in front of me. I could barely see the yellow stripes in the road. Yet I knew that the sun was shining somewhere above me, but I couldn't see that either.

Then it dawned on me (or actually I think it was probably the Holy Spirit talking to me) – this is like the relationship between me and Jesus. It's like me to get in my car and "believe" that "I" am in the driver's seat, going where "I" want to go and Jesus is going "with" me, but "I" am still driving and WHAM – there it is, the cloud that has been waiting to drop on "my" life. I start asking myself "where are you Lord? – I can't see where I am going – have you abandoned me? My life is bumpy, and curves are being tossed in front of me and everything seems so hazy… (and I shout out) **WHERE ARE YOU LORD?"**

The great news is that as I continued to drive to church, the clouds began to rise a little. The closer I got to church, the clouds got lighter and lighter. Finally, the church was only half a mile away and the cloud was totally gone. I could see again! Hallelujah! The fog was lifted, the streets were clear, I could see the yellow dividing lines in the road.

Isn't that like Jesus – HE never really left me, I was doing the "driving" through the fog, and the clouds and the choices that I made. But, HE wanted to be the one driving all along, and as I drew nearer to Him, everything became so clear. God's promise in Deuteronomy 31:8 is that *"He will never leave us or forsake us"*.... NEVER!

Today, if you are driving down that road of despair, loneliness, fear, doubt, shame, unworthiness, ugliness, un-forgiveness, selfishness, or any other road, remember that Jesus is just a glimpse behind the clouds. All you have to do is leave the driving up to Him.

****

ASK YOURSELF:

What is God revealing to me today?
_____
_____
_____
_____
_____

How do I see God working in my life today?
_____
_____
_____
_____
_____

What can I do to bring a blessing to someone else?
_____
_____
_____
_____
_____
_____

Journey Date 57_____

Sometime ago my husband I decided to "re-do" the master bedroom closet. Myhusband wanted to give the closet a make-over or in other words, restore it back to being a closet and not a "junk pile" or "collector's bin". Naturally, to do that EVERYTHING has to come out of the closet. I hate to admit this, I always say that my husband is the pack rat, but, true confession is, this time it was all me. I had clothes two sizes too small, two sizes too big (that's always a good thing), boxes of papers, the original "wedding box" (this is the box of memories from when Bill and I got hitched), shoes too small, shoes too big, shoes I haven't worn in three years…. The list could go on and on.

We finally got it all out. Bill ripped out the old shelves and put up beautiful new, white, double decked shelves. The closet seemed so much bigger and roomy. Then came the time to put everything back in the closet. You can probably guess where I am going with this… not EVERYTHING was put back in the closet. I think I had two bags of trash and old clothes that I was NOT putting back in. The trash went right where it belonged and the clothes went to a recycle container. I had so much space now that the clothes neatly hung on the racks, and the shoes are up on the shelf. As crazy as this may sound, I am really proud of my closet. My husband did an awesome job in "restoring" the old junked up closet to a beautiful, pleasant closet to walk in to. I hope to keep it this way.

It dawned on me that I am the same way with God. I store up in my mind, my heart, my body and my spirit, EVERYTHING that I have done wrong or bad or hurtful, and the place in my heart for God becomes a "collector's bin" of trash and unneeded things. I stock pile so much stuff that it is difficult for me to hear God. Sometimes I cry out to God, "aren't you listening to me?" – when in reality I should be saying - "why can't I hear you God?" After seeing the restoration of my closet, I realized that He isn't "stuffing the heart full of junk" – I am.

Psalm 51:12 says, *"Restore to me the joy of your salvation and grant me a willing spirit to sustain me."* This is what I want from God, to restore to me the joy of HIS salvation and to give me a willing spirit to keep me that way. It is difficult not to shove "junk" into the closet of our heart, but with God's power, mercy and grace He will help to restore us.

Today is your "closet" cluttered? Let God will restore HIS joy to you, and remove the "junk" from your heart.

****

ASK YOURSELF:

What is God revealing to me today?
_____
_____
_____
_____
_____
_____

How do I see God working in my life today?
_____
_____
_____
_____
_____
_____

What can I do to bring a blessing to someone else?
_____
_____
_____
_____
_____
_____

Journey Date 58_____

Have you ever made a new Resolution to change something? I try not to, because it seems that I always break them. You know, that proverbial one "I AM going to loose weight this year!" (That is the number one resolution made each year.) Then of course when you fail at keeping your resolution, you feel bad. Emotions and inside thoughts of self-condemnation and feeling like a failure show up.

Let me encourage you today to know that God never fails at His resolutions. He always comes through, even when you feel like your fire is about to go out or you are at a breaking point. He promises us in Isaiah 43:2 - *"A bruised reed He will not break and a smoldering wick He will not put out, but He will bring justice and truth."*

When you feel like your flame is dying or you can no longer keep the "resolution", God is there to hold you up and keep your fire stoked.

Maybe you are okay, but the person next to you looks like the broken reed... I encourage you to help them stand and give them a fresh drink today by your smile and your words.

Today, may the Lord restore the fire, take away the condemnation and pour His blessings upon you.

****

ASK YOURSELF:

What is God revealing to me today?

_____
_____
_____
_____
_____
_____
_____
_____

How do I see God working in my life today?

_____
_____
_____
_____
_____
_____
_____
_____

What can I do to bring a blessing to someone else?

_____
_____
_____
_____
_____
_____
_____
_____

Journey Date 59_____

Many of you have heard me talk about my German Shepherd, Charlie, and the many things that I learned from him. Well Charlie is no longer with us. For several months he began having problems walking, and then more problems with his bladder. We took him to the vet to have him checked out, only to find that he had over 20 bladder stones and acute arthritis in his back, both back hips and all of his legs. After asking the opinion of the vet of how to treat Charlie, and having Charlie in "doggie diapers" for three months and watching him cry when he went up and down the stairs, we finally decided that it was time to let him go. Charlie was 15 years old. But it was my loving husband who decided to give Charlie his "last supper", or breakfast as it may be. My husband got up and made a pan of brownies, bacon and eggs, biscuits, gravy and sausage. We sat out on the patio and had breakfast with Charlie. We gave him one of our good plates, filled it with all of the goodies and watched him enjoy every bite. He didn't know what was about to happen, but he so enjoyed the moment of being with us, outside where he loved to be, eating everything that he knew was too good to be true... especially the chocolate brownies!

Charlie has been gone now for some time. I don't know why this image has been so clear in mind lately, except that as I write it, I am reminded that Charlie lived every moment for the moment. He didn't think about "what is going to happen to me", he just loved the moment. So many times I miss the moment, because I get so caught up in the "what if's", and "what now's". I could learn a lesson from my precious Charlie... live today for today.

In *Matthew 6: 25 Jesus tells us, "do not worry about your life, what you will eat or drink, or about your body and what you will wear. Is not life more important than food, and the body more important than the clothes you wear?"*

Today as your day goes by, look for the moments of joy right before your eyes. Take a few moments and pass on your worries to God and let Him take care of you and enjoy the chocolate brownies of life.

****

ASK YOURSELF:

What is God revealing to me today?

_____
_____
_____
_____
_____
_____
_____
_____
_____

How do I see God working in my life today?

_____
_____
_____
_____
_____
_____
_____
_____
_____

What can I do to bring a blessing to someone else?

_____
_____
_____
_____
_____
_____
_____
_____
_____

Journey Date 60_____

A few years ago my step-mother gave me a book called, "90 Minutes in Heaven". She told me that once I started reading it, that I wouldn't want to stop until I got to the end. She was correct. I have heard so many stories about different people who have "died and gone to Heaven", that I wondered how this book would be any different. It was. While reading the book I thought about those loved ones that have preceded me. My mom, my father-in-law, my grandfather and grandmother, my dear friends' daughter, my two friends mother's, and so many more. After reading this book, I realized that there are no words that can bring comfort to the hurting here on earth, but oh my friend, the comfort that is in Heaven… how marvelous! No more pain. No more aches. No more sorrow. No more worry. No more debt. It truly must be a place that we cannot comprehend here on Earth, unless God chooses to let us have that "90 Minutes in Heaven", but the only way to get there is through the saving grace of Jesus.

The reason I am writing this is to ask you that one question… have you let Jesus take residence in your heart? He came and suffered here on earth, so that we would have a place of beauty to live in for eternity. I love what Jesus tells us in the book of John 10:27-30. *"My sheep listen to my voice; I know them, and they follow Me.* **I give them eternal life and they shall never perish;** *no one can snatch them out of My hand. My Father, who has given them to Me, is greater than all; no one can snatch them out of my Father's hand. I and the father are one."* Oh my friend, time is SO short

Today my prayer is that, if you have never asked Jesus to reside in your heart, that you would read these words again, and seek Him…He is waiting for you. If you do know Jesus as your personal Savior, then maybe share this message with a friend

****

ASK YOURSELF:

What is God revealing to me today?

_____
_____
_____
_____
_____
_____
_____
_____

How do I see God working in my life today?

_____
_____
_____
_____
_____
_____
_____
_____

What can I do to bring a blessing to someone else?

_____
_____
_____
_____
_____
_____
_____
_____

Journey Day 61 _____

Have you ever been in a downpour of rain? I am not sure if where you live, you have these type of rains, but up here in the Denton Country, it can pour down so hard that even my big, not afraid of anything, Samson kitty, will hide. The rains come so quickly that many of the roads flood as fast as the rain falls down. One time I decided to go out after the rains had stopped, and noticed many of the "gullies" and small creeks had risen so high that there was debris and trash all over the place. Items like old tires, metal pieces, partial fences, logs, I even saw a shoe laying on the banks of a creek. You could see how high the floods had gone with the leftover "spillage" of the water. I thought how ugly and nasty everything looked after the water had subsided.

Then it dawned on me, these "gullies" were like my mouth. No, I don't mean I have debris such as tires and shoes in my mouth, but I do have "spillage" that comes out of my mouth. Not that I want to admit that, but I do. One time I said something that I wish I had kept in my mouth, but it was too late. The flood of the words came out, and what was left behind was not pretty.

Then I found it… Jesus talking… Matthew 12:34-37 (Paraphrased) *"For out of the overflow of the heart the mouth speaks. The good man brings good things out of the good stored up in him, and the evil man brings evil things out of the evil stored up in him…But I, Jesus, tell you that men will have to give account on the day of judgement for every word they speak."* Oh Lord, forgive me… oh my friends and family, forgive me for anytime that I may have spoken words of unkindness.

Today I pray that you receive the good things that are stored up for you, and the "spillage" does not fall close to you.

****

ASK YOURSELF:

What is God revealing to me today?

_____
_____
_____
_____
_____
_____
_____
_____

How do I see God working in my life today?

_____
_____
_____
_____
_____
_____
_____
_____
_____

What can I do to bring a blessing to someone else?

_____
_____
_____
_____
_____
_____
_____

Journey Day 62 _____

Not too long ago, I went into a store and noticed that incense was burning. It has been quite some time since I burned incense, but I remember the times when I did. It was to "escape" the place that I was in and I wanted to "relax" and know that with the gentle scent I would feel like all of my troubles and fears would disappear for a while. As I stood there, I could see the small pillar of smoke making its way out of the dome like incense holder. It was a lavender scent, soft and calming, yet strong enough to make the entire place smell of this aroma.

I began to think of the wise men who brought incense to Jesus. Now what would a baby do with incense? I believe it was for Mary and Joseph to burn, to receive that calmness that the Lord had to offer them. I imagine as they burned it they gave their praises for the Savior that was born and to God Almighty who sent this little child. Though they were in an "unusual" and "difficult" circumstance, I can imagine God speaking to them, giving them a certain comfort that their prayers and concerns were being heard. Their prayers were filling the room and the Heavens above.

Psalm 141: 1-2 shows us that Psalmist cries out to the Lord... *"O Lord, I call to You; come quick to me, Hear my voice when I call to You. May my prayer be set before you like incense; may the lifting up of my hands be like the evening sacrifice."*

Then, when we think -- "God did you really hear my prayers?".... some of the most calming words are spoken back to us by our Savior, *"Come to Me, all you who are weary and burdened, and I will give you rest. Take My yoke upon you and learn from Me, for I am gentle and humble in heart, and you will find rest for your souls."* (Matthew 11:28-29) Jesus is there today, ready to give you rest as you pour out your prayers.

Today, know that your prayers are like incense to the Lord. They fill the Heavens as you cry out to Him. He loves to hear you, so keep on praying, keep on seeking, keep on believing, keep on burning the midnight oil when times are difficult, because Jesus promises us that He will give us rest.

****

ASK YOURSELF:

What is God revealing to me today?
_____
_____
_____
_____
_____
_____
_____
_____

How do I see God working in my life today?
_____
_____
_____
_____
_____
_____
_____
_____

What can I do to bring a blessing to someone else?
_____
_____
_____
_____
_____
_____
_____
_____

Journey Day 63 _____

One time I was sitting in a hotel room, in the mountains of New Mexico, and was in awe of the splendor and beauty all around me. The next day my husband and I were driving through White Sands and gazing at the mountain ranges on both sides, and a song came on from the group Mercy Me. It was a song that I heard many times before… "Word of God Speak". The song is really simple, asking God to let my words be few before Him, and that I would have ears to hear Him clearly, and that He would speak through His amazing Word.

As I listened to the words of this song, I could see God speaking through the mountains all around us. The majesty of the amazing mountains that seemed to explode out of the ground, and cause the skyline to have the handwriting of God so vivid and clear. Who else could create such an incredible vision? Who else knew exactly where to place each mountain range? Who else could catch the attention of mankind by the splendor of the mountain? It was very clear that God was showing Himself and His Word through the silence of the mountains and the movement of the winds.

Simply put, the first verse of God's word was vivid… *"In the beginning God created the heavens and the earth."* Genesis 1:1. I saw this scripture in real life. Sometimes I forget that I need to put away the noise of everyday life and remember what God did for us so long ago. Take a moment to "listen to God" and let what is around you speak clearly to you.

Today, be still and silent for a moment, and let God speak clearly to you through His creation.

****

ASK YOURSELF:

What is God revealing to me today?

_____
_____
_____
_____
_____
_____
_____
_____

How do I see God working in my life today?

_____
_____
_____
_____
_____
_____
_____
_____

What can I do to bring a blessing to someone else?

_____
_____
_____
_____
_____
_____
_____
_____

Journey Day 64 _____

At one time I worked in a finance department of a large company.. The specific department was Inventory. Each month I had to reconcile some different ledger accounts. The G/L accounts must equal all expenses that were charged against them. It really seemed pretty easy to me… most of the time. One month was a different story. There was an error. My numbers were not balancing. I began looking for the error in the files that were downloaded from our computer system. Nope, not there. Then I looked in my Excel formula's, thinking I had an error there. Nope, not there either. So I decided to start over and see if it was a "human error" that I had just missed. Still, no luck in finding the error. I highlighted columns, ran calculation's, sorted my file by dollar amounts… nothing was showing up. As much as I hate to admit it, I spent over half a day searching for this error. (Yes, I am telling on myself.)

As frustration started to set in, I heard this still small voice say… "ask **_Me_** where the error is, and I will show you." Yep, you guessed it, I listened, I asked, and within five minutes I found the error. It was such a simple error, right in front of my face. I thought to myself, "how could I have missed something so easy"? How simple it really was to find the mistake, yet I am the one that made it difficult.

Then I realized that many times I am this way with our Lord, Jesus. There are times when I feel like I have looked, and searched, and done everything in my power to get God's attention, only to realize that He is just a breath away. In Matthew 7:7 Jesus says it perfectly – _"Ask, and it will be given to you, seek, and you will find; Knock and the door will be opened to you. For everyone who asks - will receive, and whoever seeks - will find, and to him who knocks - the door will be opened."_ How simple it is when we search for our Lord. He is willing to open the door to you. Willing to give to you a new life, a new year, a new month, a new day, a new moment, all we have to do is ask.

Today, you may be in a struggling place. The struggle may seem like there is no clear answer in front of you, but God knows your heart. He will step in and open the door for you. Continue to search my beloved, for the Lord's mighty hand and His loving heart, and surely He will meet you.

****

ASK YOURSELF:

What is God revealing to me today?
_____
_____
_____
_____
_____
_____
_____

How do I see God working in my life today?
_____
_____
_____
_____
_____
_____
_____

What can I do to bring a blessing to someone else?
_____
_____
_____
_____
_____
_____

Journey Day 65 _____

I was wondering, how many of you like to go mountain climbing, or maybe rock climbing? My daughter Katy really enjoys rock climbing. She has gone with some of her friends who range in the age of 18 to 25 and they are all different shapes and sizes. Katy told me how much she really enjoyed rock climbing, even with the bruises, cuts, pains and soreness that comes along. If you have never done it, she would suggest that you climb a "rock" or take a hike in the mountain at least once. She said one of the things that was so great about rock climbing was reaching the top of the hill or mountain. Then when you get to the top of where you are climbing, it seems there is a level place to stand on. You can see how far you have climbed AND see that your friends reached the same destination as you.

Have you ever thought about the hill that Jesus had to climb up? But better yet, what about all of the different people that climbed that hill with Him? There were the centurions, the townspeople, men, women and children. There were also the High Priests and the two thieves on the crosses, and don't forget about the Scribes and the Elders of the church. Plus there was Mary, Jesus' mother, Mary the mother of James and the forgiven harlot Mary Magdalene… and of course the one man named in all four Gospels, Simon the man who carried the cross for Christ when Jesus couldn't carry it any further. **ALL** of these people "climbed the hill" but when they ALL reached the same place, it was flat and even. Everyone was equal and on level ground, with the exception of One… that was Jesus-He was above everyone, hanging on the cross.

You see, no matter who you are, where you have been, or what "status" in life you have managed to obtain or not obtain, the ground at the foot of the cross is level. We all stand in the same place before a Savior who wants to give us HIS best, HIS life, HIS grace and mercy.

To write out the story of Jesus and "the others" walking up the hill would take away from the opportunity for you to read the story yourself. I urge you to take a moment and read the last two or three chapters of Matthew or Mark or Luke or John and see the many faces of people who stood at the feet of Christ on the level ground. You are no different than any one of them. Are you the High Priest or the forgiven thief or maybe even the scorned woman who longs for forgiveness? Remember, Christ is there for you, on level ground, waiting to wrap His arms around you.

Today my prayer is that HIS blessings be poured upon each of you reading this, knowing that you are not standing on solid ground alone.

****

ASK YOURSELF:

What is God revealing to me today?

_____
_____
_____
_____
_____

How do I see God working in my life today?

_____
_____
_____
_____
_____

What can I do to bring a blessing to someone else?

_____
_____
_____
_____
_____
_____

Journey Day 66 _____

"I would sooner live in a cottage and wonder at everything, than live in a castle and wonder at nothing." - Quote by: Joan Winmill Brown

What type of house do you live in? Is it a huge house with several bedrooms, or is it a small apartment with just enough space to put everything you have in it? Or possibly a simple three bedroom, brick house in a quiet neighborhood, or maybe even in a hut in Africa. Some people are living in tents and card board boxes. Personally I live in a double-wide mobile home. Many people call them "trailers", others call it a "modular house". What I call it is "home". I read the quote above by Joan Brown and immediately thought this is exactly where I want to be. I don't want to miss out on the wonders of life.

The ultimate home that I want to live in is God's home. But, on the way I don't want to miss out on anything that HE puts before me. Sometimes the "things" that we live for, or work for get in the way of God's wonders. I know there are so many obstacles that can stop us along the way, but the "wonders" that are in front of us are just as many. One day while I was outside grilling burgers, I looked over and sitting on top of my crepe' myrtle was a baby bird. He appeared to be a "youngster". Probably just pushed out of the tree because he looked so terrified. For half an hour or so I watched this little fellow and he didn't move. What made that little baby bird sit in the tree right next to my patio? Why didn't the baby fly away? I believe it was one of God's wonders staring me right in the face. It was so small I almost missed it, but HE opened my eyes to see a marvelous sight.

What are you living for? Are you living for God's ultimate home, looking for His wonders along the way? Or, are you living day to day, in dread and suffocation of this world's stuff? Jesus gives comfort to the disciples in John 14: 1-4 - *"Do not let your hearts be troubled. Trust in God; trust also in Me. In My Father's house are many rooms; if it were not so, I would have told you. And if I go and prepare a place for you, I will come back and take you to be with Me that you also may be where I am. You know the way to the place I am going."* Isn't that wonderful, our Savior instructs us not to be troubled, because one day we will live in God's Mansion.

Today, remember to search for the wonders of life along the way.

****

ASK YOURSELF:

What is God revealing to me today?
_____
_____
_____
_____
_____
_____
_____

How do I see God working in my life today?
_____
_____
_____
_____
_____
_____
_____

What can I do to bring a blessing to someone else?
_____
_____
_____
_____
_____

Journey Day 67 _____

Have you ever had a cracked windshield? I mean to the point that it is so cracked you have to move your head around between the cracks to see where you are going? My daughter's car windshield had many cracks. The cracks were going diagonal, horizontal, at an angle, and curving every direction you could imagine. When she bought the car it had only one tiny little crack on bottom right hand side. It wasn't even noticeable. Then a rock hit the windshield and the little crack became a huge spider vein and grew and grew until looking out the front window was almost not visible. The window was replaced and wow, it was so clear. No spider veins, no cracks, nothing to peer around to try and figure out where you were driving. I didn't realize how bad the cracks were, until the new window was put in. I could see the road so clearly now.

At times we are the same way with our walk with Christ. We start out looking through a "clean window". It is easy to see where we are going, and easy to follow Christ in the direction that He is taking us. Then a little bump comes along that causes a crack in our window. The bump could be something from our past that comes back to haunt us, or a recent problem that has taken control of us. We become so involved in the problem, that the crack begins to grow. It grows to the point that the things around us become obstacles. Even our faith may become an obstacle. We try to steer ourselves down the road of life, but more "cracks" keep appearing. We wonder, whatever happened to that "clear window"? Then all of a sudden it becomes clear... we realize that we have walked away from the window that was so full of clarity. That window is Jesus. One of my favorite passages is when the Lord is talking to Moses and to Joshua. He tells them, *"I will be with you. I will never leave your or forsake you."*

When we need the clear window, when life seems full of "spider veins"... there He is, just waiting to be put in place.

Is it time to "replace" the cracked window with the original clean window and start over? Whatever your window looks like, no matter what the problem is, He is waiting to give you clarity. Call on Him today to come and give you a new view of the road that lies ahead of you.

Today is a new day, to look out the front window with clarity.

****

ASK YOURSELF:

What is God revealing to me today?

_____
_____
_____
_____
_____
_____
_____

How do I see God working in my life today?

_____
_____
_____
_____
_____
_____

What can I do to bring a blessing to someone else?

_____
_____
_____
_____
_____

Journey Day 68 _____

I was remembering when my husband and I took a trip down to Lake Houston to stay with some friends in their lake house for the weekend. It was going to be a nice relaxing weekend with no headaches, hassels or costs. Our goal was to just sit on the porch looking out over the beautiful lake. Well, you know the old saying "best laid plans go astray"...

Friday night on the way down to the city, our car began to have a problem. Bill pulled into a gas station and smoke was billowing out from the engine. We sat parked at the station for about 30 minutes, waiting for the smoke to go away so that we could see the real issue. Bill poured coolant and water into the radiator and as quickly as he poured it in, it poured out the back part of the engine and trickled down the parking lot. We were right next door to a hotel and we managed to get the car parked in the hotel parking lot. We knew we had to do something the next morning. We decided to make a trek, by foot, back to the gas station to find out if there were any local mechanics on duty in this small town.

Now the "trek" was through a soggy, stickery, tall weeds and grass, field. We headed out and began walking in two separate paths but going in the same direction. Immediately I stepped in a HUGE hole, then a mud puddle, and plenty of stickers were sticking me. So, I looked at Bill, there he was just walking with no problems. So, I decided to get back over to where he was and I followed right behind him. I stepped exactly where he stepped. He was going before me and I knew what the safe place was to step in. I don't even know if Bill knew what I was doing. But, we made it safely to the road that led to the gas station.

While I was walking behind Bill, God reminded me of the scripture in John... 8:12, *"then Jesus spoke to them again, saying, 'I Am the light of the world. He who follows Me shall not walk in darkness, but have the light of life.'"* No matter where you are standing, as long as we stand in the footsteps of Jesus there will be light. No matter where you are walking, if you walk in the path of Jesus Christ, you will have light. You may feel like you are standing in a deep fog, or a walking in mud holes, but Jesus has made this promise that we WILL have the light of life and NOT walk in darkness.

Today if you feel you are walking in darkness or in mud holes, know that you are not alone, Jesus is beside you.

****

ASK YOURSELF:

What is God revealing to me today?

_____
_____
_____
_____
_____
_____
_____

How do I see God working in my life today?

_____
_____
_____
_____
_____
_____
_____

What can I do to bring a blessing to someone else?

_____
_____
_____
_____
_____
_____
_____

Journey Day 69 _____

North Texas was receiving its fair share of rain and thunderstorms. Once when I was out of town, my husband called me and told me that he did not sleep well due to the storms. I thought for a few seconds why he didn't sleep well, then he continued to tell me that it wasn't the actual storm, but it was our 20 pound kitty, Samson that kept him awake through the night. Samson really doesn't like storms, and I must admit that I have spoiled him a little when it does storm. At the first sound of thunder or lightening, Samson is on the bed, making his way to my king size pillow to lay right next to my head. My thinking is the closer he is, the more protected he feels. The problem was that my husband was laying in my spot, so Samson took it upon himself to do what he normally does when he is afraid... lay right next to Bill's head. If Bill moved, Samson moved. If Bill rolled over, Samson scooted closer. Bill said that Samson was really afraid and shaking, but he was also annoying. Samson knew where to go when he was afraid. Samson also knew that Bill, or myself, would comfort him to the best of our "cat"ability and pet him and let him know that everything would be okay. Of course the storm lasted most of the night, so Bill didn't get much sleep, but Samson slept like a baby. He felt safe and protected.

How many times in my own life have I felt afraid of a situation that I was in, or frightened of? Like the storm that rolled in at our house, and the storms that roll into our lives, we do have a "safe place" to go. One of my favorite promises from God is in Isaiah 40:11 - He tells us, *"Fear not for I am with you. Be not dismayed for I am your God and I will strengthen you. Yes, I will help you, I will uphold you with MY righteous right hand."*

Wow, does God really and truly give us strength? Does He really help in our times of need? Will He take the fear away? These are really tough questions when you are standing in the storm. Samson knew that he would be taken care of if he just went to the right place... to the king size pillow laying next to Bill. The fear was familiar to Samson, but he remembered where to run to, in his time of fear.

Today, if you are in a place that you feel fear is standing right next to you, run to the familiar place of the "King's throne" and lay next to Him. He is there ready to hold you close and keep you safe in His righteous right hand.

****

ASK YOURSELF:

What is God revealing to me today?

_____
_____
_____
_____
_____
_____
_____

How do I see God working in my life today?

_____
_____
_____
_____
_____
_____
_____

What can I do to bring a blessing to someone else?

_____
_____
_____
_____
_____
_____
_____

Journey Day 70 _____

Have you ever lost anything? Have you ever been on a trip somewhere and left something behind? Or you planned a trip to be somewhere and you got where you were going and realized you left something at home that you desperately needed? I imagine the answer would be yes from most of us. I have done all three of these. Once I was staying in a hotel and I had taken my jewelry off and laid it on the bathroom counter. My jewelry consisted of a pair of silver hoop earrings, a pearl ring that my daughter gave me, a Sylvester watch (yes, that is Sylvester the cat) and a ring that I inherited when my mother passed away. The next day came and we left to go to our next destination.

We hadn't been there more than five minutes and my heart sank…. You guessed it, I left my jewelry sitting on the bathroom counter at the hotel. I wasn't too concerned about the watch and earrings, but both of the rings meant more to me than just being a ring. They were "heirlooms" to me. How could I have done such a ridiculous thing? What was I thinking? Didn't these "things" mean more to me than just jewelry? Of course they did but that doesn't mean I left them there on purpose. As a matter of fact, I was so excited to be able to see an old friend that day, I just wanted to get where we were going, and didn't even think about the jewelry. But when I realized what I had done, my heart sank. I ran to where Bill was and told him what I had done. He immediately called the hotel and he said he would drive back and pick up my jewelry. I waited for Bill to come back and I prayed. I asked God to please watch over these special things and to remember how "invaluable" and important they were to me. A little while later Bill walks in with the jewelry. I thanked him and thanked God for taking care of me in my time of "senselessness".

Immediately God was showing me that we do the same thing with Him. We will be going along and know that God, the Holy Spirit and Jesus Christ are with us everywhere we are. Life then gets REALLY busy, and very filled up and we keep going on the paths that seem so crazy and chaotic that we just leave Jesus behind. Then we begin to feel that feeling of "oh no, I've lost Him… how do I get Him back, where can I go look for Him?" Unlike the jewelry in the hotel, I don't think I remember the places that I have left Jesus behind. Also, unlike the jewelry in the hotel, when I do leave Him behind, he will not stay there. The jewelry couldn't follow me, but God gives us a promise in Deuteronomy 31:6 and Joshua 1:5... "I will never leave you or forsake you." Isn't that too grand! We can walk away from God, (or try to), but HE will not walk away from us, OR stay sitting on the counter. I tell you today, if you have felt like there is no way for you to reach out to Jesus, or that you have gone on a trip so far away that He couldn't find you, it is absolutely not true. Stretch out your hand to the sky and let Him touch you today.

Today, God is standing there right next to you... just slip Him on your finger, and feel His touch in your heart. He is the "heirloom" of your life, and He wants to be worn in your heart.

****

ASK YOURSELF:

What is God revealing to me today?
_____
_____
_____
_____

How do I see God working in my life today?
_____
_____
_____
_____

What can I do to bring a blessing to someone else?
_____
_____
_____
_____

After reading these life stories, I have one question left – do you know Jesus?

The Word tells us that all have sinned and fall short of the glory of God, and are justified freely by His grace through the redemption that came by Christ Jesus. God sacrificed Jesus on the altar of the world to clear the world of sin. Having faith in Him sets us in the clear. God decided on this course of action in full view of the public – to set the world in the clear with Himself through the sacrifice of Jesus, finally taking care of the sins He had so patiently endured. This is not only clear, but it's now – this is current history! God sets things right. He also makes it possible for us to live in His rightness.

If you have never asked Jesus to come into your heart, pray this simple prayer:

"Jesus, forgive me, for I am a sinner. Come into my heart and lead me each day of my life. Thank You Jesus for loving me so much that you would sacrifice Your life for me. I am Yours and You are mine today and through all eternity. Amen."

If you prayed this prayer, tell someone. Or send an email to **sandy@prodigalpublishing.today,** and we will celebrate with you.

All praises to our King!

> *"But encourage one another daily, as long as it called <u>Today</u>, so that none of you may be hardened by sin's deceitfulness."*- Hebrews 3:13.

For more information about the Journey Series Books, or volume discounts, please email **sandy@prodigalpublishing.today**. You can also purchase this book on Amazon.com or through Kindle.

Thank you for your prayers and support!

Joyfully in Him!

www.ingramcontent.com/pod-product-compliance
Lightning Source LLC
Chambersburg PA
CBHW031357040426
42444CB00005B/324